Praise for *The Dance*

Brilliant. I've never heard anything like this! Just brilliant.

Eugene H. Peterson
Author of *The Pastor, The Message* Bible
Lakeside, MT

Every couple invested in life long love will benefit from this compelling book. Paul Gauche reveals a tantalizing tale that is sure to not only inspire you in your marriage, but equip you along the way, too. Don't miss out on **The Dance of Marriage**.

Drs. Les & Leslie Parrott
#1 New York Times bestselling authors
of *Saving Your Marriage Before It Starts*
Lesandleslie.com | SYMBISassessment.com
Seattle, WA

Paul is one of the most effective marriage practitioners I know. He is driven and passionate about helping couples create great marriages. I have seen this firsthand in his work with hundreds of young married couples including my own daughter and her husband. The **Dance of Marriage** *is an inspiring and practical resource for anyone wanting to nurture their marriage and has inspired me to celebrate my own 30 years of marriage. It is the dance that you will want to keep sharing with your partner.*

Sandy Rothschiller
Pastor of Spiritual Care
Prince of Peace Lutheran Church
Burnsville, MN

This is an extraordinarily accessible piece of real, usable value for us all—a gift for all who have a stake in generative marriages. As a husband, father, and pastor, Paul weaves "real life" and Scripture into a narrative of marriage strong in counsel and rich in tender inspiration. Here is a message of "realistic hope" in which God's story, Paul's story, and our stories authentically enrich each other in an extraordinary piece of "life wisdom."

Roland D. Martinson
Professor Emeritus of Children
Youth and Family Ministry
Luther Seminary
St. Paul, MN

This fresh, creative work can help couples of all ages discover dance as the hidden language of marriage. Paul draws from a lifetime of relational and spiritual experiences to help couples keep on dancing, whether they can hear the music or not.

Pastors Kathy and Matt Valan
DreamFields Ranch
Moorhead, MN

*Over thirty years ago, I was blessed to be a part of the seminary community that watched and cheered when Paul and Nancy Lee "fell in like" and then in love, and then were married. Paul's book, **The Dance of Marriage**, is a fitting tribute to the journey of Nancy Lee and Paul, as well as to so many other journeys like theirs. Marriage is both gift and challenge, with spouses learning to dance with each other, and in the best of all relationships, with God as well. **The Dance of Marriage** invites us to consider how we are invited to risk, to pray, to trust, to share, to weep, to commit, to love, and to* *know joy and peace as God blesses and encourages us to reveal Christ to one another through the gift, and the dance, of marriage.*

Mark W. Holmerud
Bishop, Sierra Pacific Synod, ELCA
Sacramento, CA

Stories are powerful tools that penetrate past our rational mind and engage our souls, taking root, growing, and anchoring themselves in our memory. Through stories told and questions asked, Paul follows his mentor, Jesus, who spoke most often in stories (parables) and never failed to ask deceptively simple—albeit soul-piercing—questions. If you know that you and your marriage are worth more: more investment, more effort, more exploration, then this book is for you. (And by the way, Paul's exploration in the "Prologue" of the biblical wedding at Cana is alone worth the price of the book.)

Phil and Debbie Waite
Logan, Utah

The Dance of Marriage

Keeping in Step
Through the Last Song

Paul Gauche

Published by Deep River Books
Sisters, Oregon
www.deepriverbooks.com

ISBN – 13: 9781632694379
Library of Congress: 2017902731

Printed in the USA
Cover design by Robin Black, Inspirio Designs

Dedication

To Nancy Lee, love of my life, sweet bride of mine for more than thirty-four years and with whom I am endlessly blessed to be sharing the most remarkable and enduring love story. The Dance continues . . .

"If it's half as good as the half we've known, here's Hail! to the rest of the road."

Sheldon Vanauken, *A Severe Mercy*

Contents

Section Five: Miracle

Section Six: Benediction

Foreword

Come and dance in the mystery
Step by step, hand in hand in God's Story
Come and dance in the mystery
Heart to heart, side by side in God's Story

— From Handt Hanson's "Come and
Dance in the Mystery"

It happened again just yesterday. A couple from the congregation I serve, people I've known and loved for nearly a decade, announced that they are getting divorced. After 38 years they are stepping off the marriage dance floor. The news is like a rock hitting a windshield. At first there's the shock, and then the radiating cracks. Their children's grief. Their grandchildren's confusion. Their friends' sadness. And then the nagging questions. What happened? Could I have done something to prevent it? How does a love that once danced with grace and passion simply end?

As a pastor, I care deeply about marriage. I want to see committed love thrive and grow. When two people love one another not only are they fulfilled, but I believe they are bearing witness to God's love through their life together. As a husband, I want to love my wife so well that when people see us together they catch a glimpse of God's love for them and for all creation. It's an audacious goal that motivates me to practice the fundamental dance steps of marriage over and over: trust, commitment, love, and forgiveness.

Every now and again I meet a couple, watch them interact, and think to myself, "That's what I want my marriage to look like when I grow up." Paul and Nancy Lee Gauche have that kind of marriage. In them I see a reflection of God's love for me and all creation. There is both an ease and an intensity of love that flows like a current between them. They laugh easily, talk and listen deeply, and welcome others into the dance. This book is our invitation to join them.

I've had the privilege of working with Paul as a pastoral colleague for nine years, and in that time I've learned that Paul is a seize-the-day kind of guy. Paul is intent upon making the most of each day, mining the meaning from what many of us simply dismiss as the ordinary moments of life. In this book Paul challenges us to do that same work with the most important relationship in our lives: our marriage.

Paul cares deeply about marriage. He also loves Jesus, and he brings those two passions together in this book. In these pages you'll be challenged to dive deeply into the story of Jesus at the Wedding in Cana and discover some profound lessons for living into the richness of love and marriage. You'll follow the journey of Charlie and Anna, a couple preparing for the dance of a lifetime. Most importantly you'll be invited to reflect on what it means that Jesus doesn't just want to be invited to your wedding: Jesus chooses to be a partner in the dance of your marriage.

The Dance of Marriage isn't a textbook on relationships; it's a workbook for your marriage. This book doesn't just challenge us to think about marriage; it equips us to explore the depths of our partnership. Paul draws upon his pastoral work with hundreds of couples, preparing them for marriage, officiating at their weddings, and coaching them through the inevitable dips and twists of the daily dance of nurturing love. Couples young and old have learned how to dance more gracefully with their partner because of Paul's passionate work. As someone who wants to dance with my bride "until death do us part," I value the wisdom that Paul shares in this book, and I'm putting it into practice. I hope you will too.

I'm grateful for my friendship with Paul and grateful for the ministry that we get to share together. We've often joked that we are twin sons of different mothers. If we had attended middle school together we're pretty sure we'd have spent a lot of time in detention! And I'm also grateful that Paul has written this book because I dare to believe that the ancient wisdom from Scripture and current wisdom of my friend can help us all to dance with greater passion. The rhythm and rhyme of your marriage dance matters, not just to you, but to God and to a world that needs to see a reflection of God's love for them.

When ancient theologians struggled to describe the relationship between the three persons of the Trinity, they used the metaphor of a dance. At Greek weddings multiple dancers move in circles, weaving in and out, moving faster and faster in seemingly flawless synchronicity. The many appear to move as one. That, said ancient theologians, is how it is with the Trinity. Father, Son, and Holy Spirit dance as One to the rhythm of love. And we, by faith, are invited to be a part of the dance. This book is your invitation to imagine that the dance of your marriage is being woven in the larger dance of God's work in the world, "step by step, side by side, in God's story." How cool is that?

I hear music. It must be your time to dance.

Jeff Marian, Lead Pastor, Prince of Peace Lutheran Church, Burnsville, MN

Prologue

"Dad, do you know of any good books on relationships?"

I was looking into the face of a kid with a broken heart. He was hurting and desperate for some help, anxious for some insight and guidance, and longing for some relief. He was looking for a way forward, a way beyond.

Our son Soren, who was twenty-two years old at the time, was feeling the deep pain of letting go of a significant relationship and was feeling rudderless. He was adrift and searching for some resources to help him navigate the swirling waters of heartbreak and sadness as he wrestled with the sudden, gaping emptiness that was overwhelming him. We were standing together in the self-help section of a local bookstore, but for all the titles that seemed to promise a quick fix, Soren was powerless to help himself and was asking me for help. Quite honestly, at that moment I was feeling equally helpless to point him to a way forward.

It was an ironic moment. On the one hand, we were surrounded by hundreds of books; good books, even great books, each one part of a multi-billion dollar industry, each one in its own way claiming to have the "hot tip" on healthy relationships. Books with "10 Steps," "Three Ways," "5 Methods," and "Thirty Days," all promising "Stronger Relationships," "More Love," "Better Communication," "Deeper Understanding," and even "Mind-Blowing Intimacy." There would certainly be something of value in any number of those books.

On the other hand, I reminded myself that I was a leader, a teacher, a pastor in the church. I had a fairly decent handle not only on how the ancient Scriptures once spoke but also on how they continue to speak into our present-day lives, calling us to be intentional about nurturing strong relationships. The questions were swirling in my mind. *Surely, I could pull something out of that book that would be helpful to him? Couldn't I at least recommend a page, a portion from that book? Couldn't I at least recommend a passage from that ancient, centuries-old, once-spoken, still-speaking book that would speak a fresh, new, powerful, and relevant word into this twenty-first-century young man's life? Couldn't I?* I wondered. If the narratives from Scripture truly come from, as A.W. Tozer wrote in *The Pursuit of God*, "Not only a book which was once spoken, but a book which is now speaking . . . words from a God who is speaking in the continuous present,"[1] then yes, certainly I could, and should, and would, recommend that book!

I've invested in strengthening friendships, deepening relationships, and transforming marriages for more than thirty years. I've done this in the contexts of the communities where I've served as a Lutheran pastor: first in a small community in West Central Minnesota, then in a larger community in Southeastern Minnesota, and currently in the South Metro area of the Twin Cities of St. Paul and Minneapolis. I've worked with hundreds of couples planning weddings who desired to get their marriages off to a great start. I've partnered with my wife, Nancy Lee, in leading countless retreats and workshops for people wanting to be purposeful and intentional about developing their relationships. I've celebrated anniversaries and presided over renewals of vows with couples who have worked diligently to make their good relationships better and their great marriages stronger. At the same time, I've walked deeply into troubled relationships with those who have come to the end of their hopes and dreams, to the end of themselves; couples needing a fresh wind of healing from a God who blessed them to be a blessing to each other but somehow had lost sight of what that meant in their lives together.

This book aims at making strong marriages even more vital and fulfilling. Instead of quoting numerous steps, myriad ways, multiple methods, and infinite checklists (which only work for some), I'll draw significantly on a passage from Scripture that contains ancient wisdom from a first-century wedding celebration in Cana. I'll explore how that particular narrative continues to speak relevantly and powerfully to marriages today.

I'll also bring to the conversation more than thirty years of pastoral ministry helping over 400 couples "tie the knot." Certainly, thirty years of doing *anything* might, to some people, seem impressive. But just leaving an impression isn't the intention here. Mining wisdom and providing insight is the purpose. It's those insights that I've gathered and the wisdom that's grown out of my friendships with these couples that have fueled the passion for this book. While the insights from all those relationships couldn't possibly be contained in a single volume, the combined stories of hope and promise in this book will provide practical advice that will speak clearly to couples of any age preparing for a life together in a marriage.

In every relationship into which I've been invited, at some point, in some form or another, I've been asked the same question that Soren asked me in that bookstore: "Do you know of any good books on relationships?" Every time, I've wanted to hand them something like this book. Now I can. It's in your hands.

People have been embracing the journey of relationship since the dawn of time. Along the way, somewhere between trust and love, after the engagement and just before the rhythms and realities of married life begin to set in, people often gather for a celebration. There's something deeply joyful about finding the love of one's life and bringing a community together to celebrate. It's almost as if we've known from the very beginning that joining two lives together is such a wonderfully remarkable—and at the same time, remarkably challenging—undertaking that it compels people to gather together to support it, witness it, bless it, and throw a big party to rejoice over such an adventure.

Although the traditions and practices, whims and inclinations, and customs and ceremonies have varied widely through the centuries, the basic script has remained fairly intact and unfolds each time in a roughly similar fashion:

- Two people meet, and so it begins . . .
- A couple falls in love and decides to "take the plunge," "jump the broom," "tie the knot," "get hitched" . . .
- Invited guests and family members join in the celebration . . .
- A pastor, a priest, a minister, a rabbi, a judge—some designated officiant—calls things to order and offers prayers, readings, insights, exhortations, and blessings; which usually leads to a recitation of vows, or promises; after which the couple exchanges gifts (usually rings), which are visible signs of their invisible commitments . . .
- The couple "seals the deal," the contract, the covenant, with a kiss; at which point the crowd applauds "the world's most newly married couple," sending them on their merry way . . .
- Finally, off they go to the reception, where more customs and traditions are observed, including introductions of the wedding party, speeches, toasts, meals, dancing, and so forth . . .

This is, more or less, the way wedding stories play out. But we ought not to hurry along to the reception. There will be plenty of time to celebrate with the happy couple. By rushing off too quickly and partying too soon, we run the risk of missing some of the more subtle and profound moments in this unfolding excitement. So let's hold back just a bit and linger a while at the wedding itself. Let's take the time to consider a very particular wedding story preserved for us by the first-century biblical writer John, which will prove wise and insightful for twenty-first century readers. But first, a word of clarification, if not caution.

Weddings are not merely spectator events. Contrary to popular belief, to say nothing of common practice, guests are not invited to a wedding merely to watch a couple get married. Friends and families haven't made commitments of travel and time, to say nothing of financial commitments and, in some cases, very specific wardrobes, to simply witness or observe this ancient and enduring routine. There is more; so much more. There is something deeper and far more meaningful into which the guests have been invited.

By hurrying off to the reception, we can easily miss the deeper level of participation that genuinely invites us in and asks something of us. It expects, even demands, something of us for the sake of healthy and whole relationships, not to mention the wellbeing of the whole community. When we gather to celebrate a wedding, there is something that hopes—even dares—to speak into every relationship represented in the gathering of friends and family. We begin to understand the significance of the invitation to this deeper level when we engage our imaginations and peel back the layers of the ancient story of the wedding in Cana. If we fail to do this by simply rushing off to the reception, we miss what this story has to say to each one of us.

We miss how John's ancient narrative speaks into every relationship present at a wedding.

Marriages have framework and movement. From subtle beginnings all the way through to the remarkable and extraordinary richness of years together, love is forged and marriage is built on a subtle structure emerging from John's ancient story. Like six jars of water holding far more than water, this ancient framework—beginnings, celebration, crucible, counsel, miracle, and benediction—holds far more than we expect. Within this broad framework, we observe several more subtle movements, with each one building on the last. And all these movements are rooted in the seemingly innocent, often random, sometimes awkward, introductions that can lead to trust, commitment, engagement, invitation, ceremony, marriage, promises, crisis, advice, gratitude, and hope. All this opens up to the extraordinary celebration of love in the dance of life together, during which couples mark the anniversary of years of life together.

So take a few extra moments with these ancient words from John and look more closely at the story:

> On the third day there was a wedding in Cana of Galilee, and the mother of Jesus was there. Jesus and his disciples had also been invited to the wedding. When the wine gave out, the mother of Jesus said to him, "They have no wine." And Jesus said to her, "Woman, what concern is that to you and to me? My hour has not yet come." His mother said to the servants, "Do whatever he tells you."
>
> Now standing there were six stone water jars for the Jewish rites of purification, each holding twenty or thirty gallons. Jesus said to them, "Fill the jars with water." And they filled them up to the brim. He said

to them, "Now draw some out, and take it to the chief steward." So they took it. When the steward tasted the water that had become wine, and did not know where it came from (though the servants who had drawn the water knew), the steward called the bridegroom and said to him, "Everyone serves the good wine first, and then the inferior wine after the guests have become drunk. But you have kept the good wine until now."

Jesus did this, the first of his signs, in Cana of Galilee, and revealed his glory; and his disciples believed in him.

John 2:1–11 (NRSV)

This is a fabulous story, full of tension and wonder that draws us in deeper and deeper. And once we have arrived at the wedding, we're left only with John's descriptions and our imaginations. While John does provide *some* details, he does not give us *all* the details. We will do well to keep in mind that John is revealing something only our imaginations can fully grasp. As author, speaker, and theologian Brian McLaren wrote of John's unique writing style:

> Matthew, Mark, and Luke tell the story of Jesus in ways similar to one another (which is why they're often called the synoptic gospels—with a similar optic, or viewpoint). Many details differ (and the differences are quite fascinating), but it's clear the three compositions share common sources. The Fourth Gospel tells the story quite differently. These differences might disturb people who don't understand that storytelling in the ancient world was driven less

by duty to convey true details accurately and more by
a desire to proclaim true meaning powerfully.[2]

Put another way, John's narrative paints a beautiful picture
with words not merely to tell us what once happened, but rather
to challenge us to consider what continues to take place when
we're open to the narrative becoming our story.

So we can, in fact, only imagine the beginnings for this
young couple from Cana. We can only imagine how their introductions took place. Perhaps it was during a trip to the market
to gather bread, or while gathering water at a well, or at a gathering of family and friends—we can only imagine. It's enough
to say the lives of these two individuals did indeed intersect, and
their introduction was their beginning. With that the movements began, and in due time trust deepened and a commitment was made.

We can only imagine the growing excitement for the celebration to come. During the long months of engagement, the
good news spread from village to town, from one person to the
next, and plans were made for inviting family and friends to join
the ceremony. As important as it is that Jesus, his mother, and
the disciples were present at the wedding, the simple fact they
were invited is not the main point. The main point—which so
easily gets overlooked—is that Jesus, his mother, his followers,
and the rest of the guests were invited to the crucible of this
couple's marriage.

There is a profound difference between the two; a difference we must not miss. The couple's *wedding* was something
celebrated on a particular day at a particular time in a particular
place. Their *marriage*, on the other hand, was something that
would unfold along the way, over time, again and again beyond
historical, linear, and chronological time. While their wedding

was certainly rooted in their past, growing into that one present moment, their marriage would extend into their future
together. And it would be there, in the steady rhythm and reality of the daily-ness of their marriage together, that their promises once made would become promises continually kept. This
would provide support for the weight of crisis when it arrived—
because crisis always arrives. We can only imagine.

In John's telling of the story, the wine runs out. This was a
big problem. Running out of wine was, in a word, catastrophic.
As sometimes happens when families and friends gather to celebrate, and in spite of the best planning, the crisis of running out
of wine threatened the whole enterprise as it was coming to its
culmination. The wedding day for this up-and-coming young
couple was in danger of going down in local, if not theological,
history as a debacle of biblical proportions.

"They have no wine. . . ."

Four more wretched words could not have been spoken.
Four words: pronoun, verb, adjective, noun—barely a sentence,
but completely disastrous. And if not for Jesus' presence that
day, it would have been a sentence of guilt and shame pro-
nounced on the couple and their families from that day forth
and evermore. Thankfully, in this case, crisis turns to counsel.

Jesus' mother provides the counsel. Mary gives the advice
of the ages, which gives way to gratitude, which creates hope.
In the midst of the crisis, Mary turns to the servants and speaks
five words that changed the course of that day and impacted the
lives and relationships of every couple who has ever dared to
heed them since: "Do whatever he tells you."

Perhaps the surprise in all this is simply found in the servants' obedience, however hesitant, to Jesus' direction. This
instruction comes quickly after his seemingly odd response
to Mary's plaintive summary of the situation: "Woman, what

concern is that to you and to me? My hour has not yet come." After all, what else could the servants do? With a wedding and a reception for who-knows-how-many guests teetering on the brink of utter disaster, to say nothing of a family's honor on the line, the servants simply did as they were told:

"Fill the jars with water."

But wait. There must have been some skepticism. We can only imagine. Can't we almost hear them scoffing under their breath? Can't we almost read their minds as they look incredulously at one another? "Fill the jars with *what*? Did he say fill the jars with water? Is he serious? The guests will be disappointed when they learn the wine has given out—but now we're going to mock them by serving . . . water?"

Everything about these two instructions—first from Jesus' mother, "Do whatever he tells you," and then from Jesus himself, "Fill the jars with water"—would have likely seemed ridiculous to the servants. We can only imagine. But Mary trusts Jesus. And the servants, though mostly dubious about the whole mess, do as they are told. If crisis turns to counsel, then this is where advice leads to gratitude and hope. And hope points to something like a miracle.

Then the miracle begins to unfold. In the presence of Jesus, "six stone water jars each holding twenty or thirty gallons" of water becomes wine. Quite a lot has been made of the amount of wine produced on that particular day, at that particular time, in that particular place. Intricate, if not entertaining, mathematics have been employed to produce sufficient awe in the reader over how much water was fermented—as if Jesus wasn't completely able to turn every drop of liquid in the whole country into something other than what it was.

Yet in the end, the amount of wine produced that day does not matter. The point John makes as he spins out his wonderful narrative is simply this: where Jesus is invited, even in the abundance of nothing, there remains a promise of something. Where Jesus is invited, even in overwhelming scarcity, there is a possibility of sufficiency. Where Jesus is invited, even in the glare of impossibility, there is the hope of abundance.

Finally, there is a blessing—a benediction—that seems to flow out of these six stone water jars into the lives of the bride and groom, their families, their friends, all who looked on, all who entered in, and all who have ever since come into the promise of that wedding in Cana. The first-century framework still stands. It stands for every person seeking stronger friendships, deeper relationships, and transformed marriages. And the movements that began with a wedding in Cana of Galilee continue to move in the twenty-first century.

Section One

Beginnings

On the third day there was a wedding in Cana of Galilee . . .

John 2:1

1

Introductions

"I cannot fix on the hour, or the spot, or the look, or the words, which laid the foundation. It is too long ago. I was in the middle before I knew that I had begun."

—Jane Austen, *Pride and Prejudice*

Except for a chance meeting that would alter my life forever, it was just another ordinary weekday morning. The chapel service at Luther Seminary had ended, and I was walking back to my dorm to retrieve my backpack for another full day of classes. I had planned my day. My schedule was set, and I was ready to go. That's when I heard someone call my name.

"Hey, Paul!"

I turned and saw my good friend Bill, whom I had met the previous year, in the crowd of students behind me. Bill was from Williston, North Dakota, and I was from Seattle, Washington. I had already introduced him to a few of my friends from the West Coast. Bill was now about to introduce me to a friend of his from the Midwest.

"Wait up a minute," Bill said.

I stopped at the top of the steps leading into the dorm, turned around, and waited for him to catch up. I didn't recognize the cute girl walking with him, but it was fair to assume, based on their animated conversation and easy laughter, that they were good friends.

I was in the middle of the third week of classes during my second year at Luther Theological Seminary. Just enough time had passed for me to get used to the rhythm of life in graduate school: wake up, eat, attend classes, take notes, read, work, study, work out, write, type, sleep, shower, rinse, and repeat. It had become a very familiar rhythm.

But that rhythm was all about to change.

"I want you meet someone," Bill said, now halfway up the steps. "Paul, this is Nancy Lee. Nancy Lee, this is Paul."

"Hey, Nancy Lee," I said, extending my hand toward her as she and Bill neared the top step.

"Hi Paul," she replied, smiling. She reached out her hand to take mine, but then missed the top step, stumbled on it, and lurched forward. It wasn't planned, of course, because it couldn't have been planned any better. And to be honest, there isn't any better way to describe what happened next than just to say I caught her. I simply caught her.

In the years following this event, variations of this story have emerged, each with a little more embellishment, each with a little more color commentary than the last.

"She fell into my arms!"

"She stumbled into my life!"

"She tripped up!"

I've told this "introduction story" so many times that the memory of the experience runs the risk of being eclipsed by the memories of retelling it. To be sure, a bit of revisionism has certainly taken over by now. But whatever version most resembles the actual event, the simple truth remains that at about eleven o'clock on the morning of September 30, 1981, Nancy Lee and I were introduced to one another outside Stub Hall on the campus of Luther Theological Seminary. She tripped on the top step, stumbled forward, and I caught her. And while it's equally accurate to say that she caught me, the joy and the mystery of what began on that top step with a simple—if not awkward—handshake has resulted in an embrace that has endured and matured and is now growing into its fourth decade.

Nancy Lee and I announced our engagement just a few months later. Our families and friends were thrilled to celebrate with us. And then, several months after that, on a hot, dusty, dry summer's evening on the last day of July in Williston, North Dakota, Nancy Lee and I stood on the top step of the chancel in her home church, faced each other, and spoke these promises:

> *The journey toward becoming one with you is an adventure in faith, a celebration of new life, and a joy beyond anything I've ever known. You are a gift from God to me. And before God and in the presence of our families and friends gathered here to celebrate with us, I commit myself to you with these promises. I love you, and I want to share my life with you. I promise you my love and faithfulness, my respect and commitment to serving you in love as Jesus has taught us to serve. I commit to you all that I am and promise to be your best friend in all our joys and sorrows, laughter and tears, as we seek to glorify our Lord. With God's help, I commit myself to being your needs fulfilled as we share in the fullness of life together. I take you with great joy to be my love! In Jesus' name!*

As we stood there with our closest friends at each side and our families gathered around us, we had no idea what lay ahead. We didn't know what joys would overwhelm us or what challenges would undermine us. We didn't know what laughter would loosen us or what tears would toughen us. There was no way we could have known what headaches would pound away on us or what heartbreaks would galvanize us. We didn't know what blessings we'd multiply or the sadness we would divide by sharing them together.

There was so much—*too* much—that we simply could not know. Yet in the face of all that we did not know, three things remained: we knew we had each other, we knew God had us, and we knew that was enough. And without much of a strategy for how we would proceed, but with an abundance of passion, determination, and modeling from our families, we ran headlong into that hot, dusty, dry day in Williston and into the weeks, months, and years beyond. We knew we had each other, we knew God had us, and we knew that was enough.

For more than thirty-four years, that's remained enough as we've worked to figure out our roles along the way. There are more than enough metaphors for that: Nancy Lee is the string; I am the kite. She's the rudder of the boat; I'm the wind in the sails. She is the left brain; I am the right. She balances the books and pays the bills; I do my share to create imbalance with spending habits (especially when it comes to kitchen tools, gadgets, and cooking gear). Yet all of that somehow drives us together—even now. In spite of how wildly different we're wired and how uniquely we've been created, we're more committed than ever to weaving our lives together as we continue to discover how to be married and model that for our family and friends.

That's been enough as we've learned, and relearned, how to talk and to tangle, how to negotiate and to listen, how to love and to serve, and how to forgive and to live together. Now, all these years later, we continue to hold fast to what's always held us together. We know we have each other, we know God has us, and we know that's enough.

Of course, that's not to say that Nancy Lee and I have a corner on the kind of love that grows, endures testing, and matures through the years. Couples have been experiencing this kind of love since the beginning of time. In fact, once upon a time, a young couple from the town of Cana fell in love. While we can only speculate about most of the details, we can safely assume that in that ancient village in northern Israel near Nazareth, in the region of Galilee, the young couple gathered their families together and invited their friends to add their blessing to the great adventure of marriage to which they must have sensed God calling them.

For several days on end they celebrated. They looked back at what had brought them together and looked ahead to the adventure that stretched out in front of them. Together they bravely leaned into that day and, presumably, each new day thereafter, trusting their commitment to each other. They had, mostly likely, been introduced to one another within the wider context of a caring, nurturing community. They didn't know what lay ahead of them, but they knew they had each other, they knew God had them, and they knew that was enough.

But time has a way of blurring the past and the earliest memories of our relationships. Often, the most significant bonding moments get lost in the clouds of history, and the very things that drew us together become the very things that pull us apart. Couples falling in love enjoy talking about how opposites attract. It's natural to be excited about something new, different, and even challenging. But it's rarely the list of opposites that keep us interested in each other. On the other hand, these things can actually become points of contention.

I can't recall a single time I ever said to myself, *Wow, Nancy Lee is so different from me. I just love that her whole family gets together on Christmas Eve and opens gifts. It's so unlike my family, where we opened gifts on Christmas Day with an intimate family gathering. I just can't wait to talk about how opposite we are!* On the other hand, it's usually the similarities, the common experiences and shared values that keep us coming back.

As relationships grow through the years, we have to learn new skills to help us navigate the embedded behaviors that cause friction and begin to drive us a little crazy about each other. While it's so easy to focus on the differences (she's right brained, I'm left brained; she stays up late, I get up early; she squeezes the toothpaste from the bottom, I just squeeze it from the middle) it's often helpful to be reintroduced to the things that drew us together. Something significant happens when we take the time to revisit the thrill of beginnings and think back on the revelry we enjoyed at the outset.

This Love of Ours . . .

Couples who come to me for guidance in rebooting their relationships often get my best advice in the form of a challenge that continues to be a great practice in healthy relationships. Think back to the earliest weeks of your relationship. You remember, don't you? It's when time seemed to stand still; when you could have stayed up for days on end by sheer will. It's when you tried holding back the nights by sharing your hopes and dreams with the other person. It's when you wove stories of what life was like before you met and discussed what it might be like to create a life together.

Try to recapture a bit of how you felt at that time. What did you laugh about together? If there were tears, what did you cry about? What did you willingly, joyfully, give up and sacrifice for each other? Reminisce a bit about the day you were introduced. Try to go back to that very moment in time when you first looked at each other, heard each other's voices, and touched each other. What were the circumstances surrounding that meeting? Where did you meet? Who introduced you to one another? What do you remember about each other? If you had the moment to do over, what would you keep the same and what would you change? Are you still in touch with the person who introduced you? What would happen if, in a spirit of gratitude and thankfulness, you reconnected with that person and simply said thank you?

There is a good chance that what brought you together and, in large part, what has kept you together are the things that you shared in common. Similar views, shared goals and values, and common experiences of joy and even sorrow are all part of the "ties that bind" us to one another. It's normal and natural for us to recount and celebrate these things. On the other hand, it's equally normal for us to want to shy away from focusing on how we are different. But differences in relationships aren't always a detriment. Differences in relationships can be seen as creating healthy tension that make us better together than we are on our own.

Next, take some time to talk with each other about your differences. As you do, keep in mind those differences may actually be complementary. Instead of turning differences into points of contention (*Why can't he just squeeze the toothpaste from the bottom like everyone else does? Why can't she just switch it up and open gifts on Christmas Eve instead of Christmas Day? Is that such a big deal?*), try to frame them as complementary. Really, how a person squeezes the toothpaste doesn't have to be a deal breaker.

Doing this might help you return to that place where you didn't know what lay ahead for you as couple—that place where you knew you had each other, you knew God had you, and you knew, somehow, that was enough.

It was just enough for Charlie and Anna.

It was evident from my first meeting with this couple that their relationship was a thrill for both of them. Anyone near the coffee shop that morning would have known it just by looking at them. There was friendship and joy, deep connection and trust, passion and commitment, and contentment and love. To say Charlie was head over heels in love with Anna would be an understatement. To say Anna was captivated with the man who sat beside her would simply be too measured. As the three of us talked together about their wedding plans, their excitement was palpable. Charlie looked at Anna, his eyes dancing with delight. Anna looked back at Charlie with just a touch of reserve, which only slightly masked her exuberance.

Planning their wedding provided about as much fun as I've had with any couple. Over the next few months, at numerous tables in several coffee shops, with more cups of coffee than I can recall, we talked about their life together: how they met, who introduced them, their hopes and dreams, their faith and love, their joy and pain, and their laughter and grief. Because Charlie and Anna also shared a component of spirituality together, we talked about the mystery of how God weaves peoples' stories and lives together and creates the marvelous architecture of marriage. We talked about the beginnings they had experienced and the crucible of bringing together two lives and weaving them into one. We talked about the counsel they had received from friends and family. And we talked about the miracle of creating life together. Charlie and Anna and I talked about the movements within this architecture—the movement of introductions, trust, commitment, engagement, invitation, ceremony, marriage, promises, crises, advice, gratitude, hope, the extraordinary, receptions, love, anniversaries, and the dance of years into life together!

I was invited into their story and into their lives to see just what made their love so remarkable. The beginning of our friendship was just a glimpse of the deep trust and commitment they shared. As I looked across the table at this couple, engaged on every level, I knew theirs would be no ordinary wedding, because this was no ordinary couple. I knew theirs would be no ordinary marriage, because this was no ordinary love. Certainly they were preparing for a wedding day. But more than that, they were preparing for a marriage together.

No one near that coffee shop that morning could have possibly known, just by looking, how utterly important that would become for the two of them.

2

Trust

"First comes love, then comes marriage . . ."

—Playground Song

Let's just get right to the heart of the matter: love does not come first. Trust comes first. And after trust has settled in, then comes love. Until trust is in place, love doesn't really stand a chance.

A lot of important pieces need to be put in place between trust and love. All kinds of essential elements must be linked together to make sure that trust gets deeply connected to love. Like pieces of a jigsaw puzzle spread out on a large table, communication, honesty, integrity, grace, and others like them must find their way into the larger picture of a relationship. But there is risk involved. There is *always* risk. Vulnerability, honesty, trust, and fear, to name a few, are the high stakes between trust and love.

It was early in the first weeks of our budding romance that Nancy Lee and I took a risk together. We did something that in certain contexts might have led to negative consequences. It was something we've since cautioned others about—especially young people getting into new relationships. Looking back I know now that it was hasty, and we did it without really thinking or even considering the consequences. But I was so excited about this girl! I was so thrilled about being with her that when I was with her I didn't want to leave, and when I wasn't with her I couldn't wait to be together. So we took a risk, threw caution to the wind, and ran headlong into the decision. We traded phone numbers. If that weren't enough—and it wasn't—we gave each other our respective addresses to where we lived.

Okay, I admit this sounds trivial. Given our twenty-first century context, where we have more access to more information more readily and more rapidly than ever before, to say nothing of how social attitudes and practices have evolved, exchanging contact information seems innocent enough. Of course, in many cases a level of caution is prudent. But there's far more going on in that moment than simply trading information. Let's pause for a moment and consider the simple act of trading "contact" information and what an act of trust this really is.

By trading phone numbers and addresses, Nancy Lee and I were giving each other access to a deeper level of relationship—the deeper level called *trust*. Think of it this way: Nancy Lee had to trust the guy that she had just met and to whom she was giving personal information was trustworthy, safe, and wouldn't use that information in a way that could jeopardize her in any way. In most cases, trading cell phone information just furthers the thrill of getting to know someone. But ultimately, handing each other our contact information provided just that: *contact*. On a far more profound level, Nancy Lee and I were also handing each other a part of our hearts and a good amount of trust that could lead to commitment.

Thankfully, in our case, it did.

We can only wonder how trust might have grown between the young couple from Cana. We can only speculate about the kind of "contact information" they might have shared with each another as their friendship grew in those first days, weeks, and months. It was a different time, to be sure, and the influence of their tight-knit community would have played a vital role in the development of their relationship. Yet, though the times were different, many of the things that deepen trust between people remain the same.

When Charlie, Anna, and I sat down to begin planning their wedding, I asked if they could pinpoint a moment in time when trust entered their relationship. Instead of identifying a particular day, a particular time, or a particular place, they mentioned several things they were doing to intentionally build trust together. Specifically, they spoke about communication, honesty, integrity, and grace.

Communication remains at the heart of growing trust. Charlie and Anna were intentional about sharing the remarkable narratives of their lives with each other. They knew that sharing all the little pieces of hope, expectation, promise, fulfillment, dreams, desires, likes, and dislikes would strengthen their trust in each other. They especially knew that being open about their vulnerabilities and weaknesses, including their own liabilities and brokenness, would develop a deeper relationship and strengthen the trust between them.

Honesty between two people is like mortar in a brick wall. It is like grout that locks floor tiles together and binds tiles of a wall into one beautiful whole piece. Honesty holds all the individual pieces together and creates strength in the structure of a relationship. After three decades of married life together, Nancy Lee and I can trust each other on levels we never dreamed possible when we began our relationship. This is precisely because we've practiced honesty with each other. Honesty, then, continues to build our growing foundation of trust.

Integrity was another characteristic that Charlie and Anna built into their life together. Regardless of what a couple wears on their wedding day—however formal or informal, plain or elaborate, unique or otherwise—it's what's on the inside that counts. I asked Anna to tell me one of the things she trusted and admired most about Charlie. She looked across the table at him and replied, "His integrity." When I asked her to say more about that, she looked at Charlie and said, "He's the same on the inside as he is on the outside."

One of the most helpful illustrations of integrity comes from the ancient craft of creating pottery. Long ago when earthenware was fired in kilns, there was always the possibility that there would be damage in the process. Clay pots, along with bowls, plates, pitchers, and drinking cups, would emerge from the ovens looking intact. But closer inspections would often reveal fissures, cracks, and other imperfections. Dishonest merchants, attempting to sell these compromised containers to unsuspecting buyers in the public marketplaces, would coat the imperfections with melted wax to hide the blemishes.

For the buyer, the test was to hold the clay vessel up to the light, which revealed its true integrity. Relationships built with integrity can stand being held up to the light. Relationships with integrity have consistency of actions, principles, values, and expectations. These are the characteristics that build trust in relationships. A relationship built with integrity looks the same on the outside as it is on the inside.

Charlie and Anna talked about the grace they had discovered in each other. The power of forgiveness had set them free to experience new dimensions of love.

When Jesus finished speaking to the disciples about the necessity and power of forgiveness, they were still scratching their heads. They likely urged Peter to ask the follow-up questions. So Peter pulled Jesus aside and asked if there was a limit to the number of times he had to forgive, adding, "As many as seven times?" You might think Peter would have shot higher than seven, but then the biblical writer Matthew had a bit of an agenda. And just for fun, let's keep in mind that Matthew, being a professional tax collector, loved playing with numbers.

According to some early Jewish traditions, a person could be forgiven up to three times for the same offense. But after that it was rather dicey; the offended person did not have to forgive the fourth time, as this was clear evidence the offending person hadn't sufficiently changed his or her ways. In light of this, Peter's response shows a great amount of generosity. But when Jesus responded to Peter with "seventy-seven times," it was another example of the call to show extravagant grace. Jesus was essentially saying there is no end to forgiveness and mercy. Grace is, by its very nature, endless. Grace that isn't endless is not grace.

This Love of Ours . . .

I've asked couples if they have secrets they keep from one another. I'm not talking about birthday gifts or Christmas present secrets that, in the end, bring joy. I'm talking about secrets that, if revealed, would cause damage to the relationship. Secrets are almost never helpful. Take a few moments and consider the secrets you have in your relationship. Ask yourself what might happen if you divulged that secret, and consider what it would do to your relationship. If there are secrets that could harm your relationship, consider talking with someone who can help you navigate through the choppy waters of communication and honesty.

You cannot overestimate the value of commitment to communication, honesty, integrity, and forgiveness in a relationship. Deeper communication will take place only as you establish a deeper level of honesty. In turn, that will strengthen the integrity of your relationship. All of this, then, along with the healthy practice of forgiveness, builds deeper trust. So talk together about the level of trust in your relationship. Go back to the beginning and discuss the things that gave you a sense that trust was beginning to grow. When you've hit those inevitable places where trust seems to be in jeopardy, ask what caused that to happen. Have you talked through those issues? How did you reconcile them? What was it like to regain trust in one another?

As I looked across the table at Charlie and Anna, I knew I was seeing a content couple who were confident and secure with each other and deeply committed to the direction of their relationship. They were sure that even though they were still learning to communicate, they had a level of honesty that supported the weight of more meaningful conversations. They were secure with each other because they trusted each other's integrity and granted each other grace by practicing forgiveness.

They told me they were intentional about these things in their relationship. They said the more they paid attention to these things, the more they trusted one another. And the more they were able to trust one another, the stronger their commitment grew. And the stronger their commitment grew, the more love they experienced for one another. Once again, I knew theirs would be no ordinary wedding, because this was no ordinary couple. I knew theirs would be no ordinary marriage, because this was no ordinary love.

I sat back in my chair, looked across the table, and thought, *Here is a couple who is wise beyond their years. Even at this early stage of their relationship, they had insight into the importance of building trust together that would take them far in their life together.*

How could I possibly have known?

3

Commitment

"Pooh!" he whispered.
"Yes, Piglet?"
"Nothing," said Piglet, taking Pooh's paw.
"I just wanted to be sure of you."

— A.A. Milne, *The House at Pooh Corner*

A journal entry:

Thoughts on the First Sunday in Advent, December 6, 1981

The season of Advent is about waiting. Advent is about waiting for the long anticipated promise-of-God-in-the-flesh to appear. But it's not a passive waiting; it's not just "waiting around for something to happen." There is an active quality to Advent waiting. Though more quiet and reflective, the season of Advent is a sitting-on-the-edge-of-your-seat kind of waiting. It's waiting filled with hope and expectation.

There is wonder.

There is reverence.

There is awe.

And then, there's just being blown away.

Nancy Lee and I had known each other for a little more than two months; the calendar had just turned to December. Add to our developing relationship two busy seminary routines filled with classes, lectures, papers, exams, work, and homework, not to mention all the driving back and forth across town to spend time with each other, and it was a busy, fast-paced, noisy, and cluttered time. This is pretty much the antithesis of what the season of Advent is all about.

But as afternoon began to turn to evening that one Sunday in December, something else began to take place. Here's how I recall what happened.

Nancy Lee and I were sitting together on the couch in her apartment. We lit the first of the five candles on the Advent wreath—four purple tapers surrounding one pink candle in the middle—and began reading a reflection for the First Sunday in Advent. When I finished reading, I closed the book, set it aside, took a deep breath, and sat back.

At first, I was simply aware of how still the room had become. It seemed like an appropriate amount of stillness for all that was going on around us in the dormitory. Yet I was becoming less and less aware of the muffled sounds of the building: students in the hallway, people in the room next door. Even the odd bump and hiss of the radiator seemed to be getting farther away.

After some moments, I gradually became more aware of breathing: my breathing, and Nancy Lee's breathing. I was aware of the rhythm of our breathing together. As the candle flickered, I slowly reached over to take hold of Nancy Lee's hand. In that moment of stillness, I was aware mostly of Nancy Lee. Warmth. Hands. Fingers. Breath. Presence. Stillness. Then the stillness began to give way to what I can only describe as a beautiful, emerging quiet—which, in the moments that followed, slowly and purposefully became something beyond quiet: *silence*.

Nancy Lee and I sat together in the large silence. For a time that couldn't possibly have been measured in linear terms, we just sat in the enveloping silence that seemed to swallow the whole room and us with it. Then, just when it seemed as if it couldn't get any more silent, it did. It became something more. Deep. Rich. Enveloping. Vast. Beautiful. Profound. Transcendent. Silent. Advent.

Nancy Lee and I sat together in the silence for a long time. For how long, I can't tell you, but what I can say is that somewhere in the midst of that deep, silent moment, I knew I was committed to Nancy Lee. The deep, rich, enveloping, vast, beautiful, profound silence of that Advent moment ushered in an anticipation of the hope and promise of things to come. I had an overwhelming confidence that whatever trust had been growing out of the beginning we had experienced on the day we were introduced had now grown into commitment.

I am the first to admit that moments and experiences like that are rare. They are few and far between, and some people never experience anything remotely similar—nor, perhaps, would they care to do so. Quite honestly, the possibility exists that over time, embellished versions of the original are created. Such is not the case with my Advent story.

But it does raise some good questions.

When does commitment happen? How does commitment take place? Can you really know when, or even if, commitment has taken root, let alone made? Can you know you're really committed to something or someone once and for all? Or is commitment something that comes and goes, ebbs and flows, and happens again and again? And to take this a step further, if commitment comes and goes, is it really commitment?

I asked Charlie and Anna about their commitment to each other. I asked when they thought they had arrived at that moment in their relationship and if, indeed, that moment could be determined at all. We wondered that if it wasn't love that came first, was it then trust that became the soil out of which their love for each other was emerging? And if that were true, wasn't it also true that their commitment to each other comes next?

In the end, we conceded that as mysterious, marvelous, holy, and splendid as love is—which, while part of some bigger architecture, still does not follow a linear pattern or emerge from a formula—there remains a kind of movement in which one thing being built on the next leads to something even more profound called *commitment*. But when does commitment take place? Is it during a long walk on the beach, during an easy run along the lake, while cross-country skiing in the park on a snowy afternoon in December? When? Is it over a lovely dinner, sharing a glass of wine, sipping a beer, eating ice cream? Is it during a first kiss? Or after? Or before? When?

This Love of Ours . . .

Consider your own relationship and think back to those first months, weeks, and even days together. What memories come to mind of the beginnings of your commitment? Can you pinpoint the first inklings of an awareness of the two of you as individuals moving toward the two of you together? How did that happen? What took place?

Couples who practice such "relational reminiscing"—that is, recalling the significant moments that strengthened their commitment to one another—discover that doing so strengthens their commitment. Are you aware of any "Advent Moments" in your relationship? Any moments that seemed sacred, or set apart, somehow? Where are those places in your relationship? How might you intentionally work toward creating more of those sacred spaces and places into the rhythm of your life together?

Charlie and Anna didn't know for sure when their commitment to one another first emerged. When I asked them, Charlie said, "It just happened." I looked at him and asked, "What do you mean, 'It just happened'? It happened, and you weren't really aware of it happening? Or, 'It just happened,' like it's just happening right now?"

What happened next was rather startling. Charlie looked at me, and then looked at Anna. Anna looked at Charlie, and then they both looked at me. Then—no kidding—both of them, at the same time, simply said, "Yes!"

Section Two

Celebration

The mother of Jesus was there. Jesus and his disciples had also been invited to the wedding.

John 2:1–2

4

Engagement

"Gravitation is not responsible for people falling in love."

—Albert Einstein

It was a chilled and wintery Saturday morning when Jake popped the question. "Can our dog be in the wedding?"

Abby and Jake were exactly three months away from their wedding day. The three of us were meeting to begin planning their ceremony. We were sitting next to the fireplace in the crowded coffee shop when Jake's question rolled out.

Well, this is a first, I thought as I sipped my coffee. I'd never been asked this specific question before. I had considered all kinds of variations on a theme with couples who wanted to express their creativity, but never this particular request.

I'd said yes to a four-year-old ringbearer pulling an infant flower girl down the aisle in a red wagon. I had delighted in the idea of a sanctuary filled with mitten-clad cross-country ski enthusiasts shaking sleigh bells instead of clapping after the introduction of the world's most newly married couple. I'd even agreed that planting a tree during an outdoor wedding after the rings were exchanged was a creative and deeply meaningful alternative to lighting a unity candle. But I had never been asked if a dog could join the wedding party.

"We'd like to have him bring in the rings," Jake continued.

"Well, that sounds interesting," I said. "Tell me more. Why is this important to you?"

Jake said that on the day they were engaged, he and Abby had planned a long afternoon at the park. The sun-drenched fields were full of happy people throwing Frisbees and footballs, flying kites, and even napping in the lazy afternoon. Picnic tables were laden with everything from pies and watermelons to beverages and condiments. The aroma of charcoal, hot dogs, brats, and burgers wafted through the air.

Jake and Abby had packed their own picnic basket and brought softball gloves and a softball. They had also brought Jake's springer spaniel, Dakota, who was doing a fabulous job of attracting attention as he darted around, chasing a tennis ball. Finally, Jake and Abby sat down on the blanket that Jake had packed. Abby gave the command for Dakota to sit.

It was only a few moments later when Abby, while petting Dakota behind the ears, let out a startled shriek. People turned to look. Abby let out another burst of delight and jumped to her feet. She covered her mouth with her hands, looked at Dakota, then at Jake, then back at Dakota, and then back at Jake again. Tears of joy mingled with laughter as Abby discovered the diamond engagement ring that Jake had bravely attached to Dakota's collar.

With Abby still in a jumble of disbelief and thrill, Jake got down on one knee. Then, with a small enthusiastic crowd looking on, he proposed to Abby. He then took the ring from Dakota's collar and slipped it onto Abby's finger. He stood up and embraced Abby as the applause rippled through the crowd that had paused to watch this unfold. At that moment, Jake and Abby, right there in the park, were sealing their relationship by giving and receiving a ring, a visible sign of the invisible covenant and relationship-promise the two of them had already begun to forge together. For Abby and Jake, the love that had grown out of trust and into commitment was seeking some kind of expression.

As the fire crackled in the fireplace and the baristas called out more orders, Abby set her tea on the table in front of her. She wrapped both hands around it, warming herself, and then sat back against the chair. She seemed more at ease now that there was at least some context to their request. "Since Dakota played such an important role in our engagement," she said, "it only seems fitting that he would deliver the ring at our wedding. So, what do you think?"

I was thinking that if they had put this much effort and emotion into choosing their K-9 ringbearer, I couldn't wait to see what the cake looked like! Then the thought occurred to me that Saint Francis of Assisi, the patron saint of animals and preacher to all creatures great and small, would have welcomed animals to a wedding. So, taking one more sip of coffee, I looked across the table at Abby and Jake, smiled, and said,

"Sure. The dog can be in the wedding."

Centuries earlier, a young couple from the town of Cana in Galilee had experienced those first mystical moments called "beginnings." They had invested in each other over time and, as a result, trust had been planted and was beginning to take root. Out of their growing trust emerged a deepening sense of commitment, which finally found its expression in their engagement.

Of course, we can only imagine how all this might have transpired between this young couple. For the most part, the story in John's Gospel only allows for our imaginations to take over when we consider this couple. We can only imagine the two of them there in that moment. We can only imagine the very moment in time when the young man from Cana realized the love that he had for the young girl across town and the place that she held in his heart. We can only imagine their families loving and supporting them to this point.

Once the decision had been made to pursue marriage, the custom of their culture suggested that the father of the young man would approach the father of the young woman with the marriage proposal. A discussion between the two fathers would have followed, and would have likely included all kinds of details. This would have included a dowry—a gift offered for the bride's hand in marriage.

It is essential to note, however, that while the two fathers played important roles in such decisions, and while the culture may have seen this as an "arranged marriage," the union was neither forced nor coerced. No one was made to wed someone whom he or she did not wish to marry. An "arranged marriage" reflected the deeper bonding that was taking place—most notably the entrusting of the bride to the groom and his family.

The pledge that was taking place had a present and ongoing nature to it, and the love, commitment, and support of entire families played an important role in the union. At some point, the groom and the bride would have been invited to join the two fathers in the conversation, with the groom announcing his love for his bride-to-be. And then, in the presence of the two fathers and his future bride, the groom would have asked her to marry him.

Again, we can only imagine the words rolling out of his mouth—words he'd privately rehearsed and was now publically exclaiming in real time to the rhythm of a pounding heart. In the presence of family members, he proclaimed, "I love you, and I want to marry you and be your husband. Will you marry me and be my wife?"

This wasn't always a "done deal." The young woman had the opportunity to decline. If she did, everything would come to a screeching halt, much to the disappointment of others in the room (including the likely humiliation of the young man).

But as the story of the couple in Cana unfolds, we know the young woman *did* accept the proposal. In a moment of sheer wonder and joy, the young man likely revealed a gift—perhaps a ring, and perhaps not, depending on the economic status of the families. Some history and tradition suggest that in the end, the young man, according to the custom and in the presence of at least two other people, would have said this to his now bride-to-be: "You are consecrated unto me . . . according to the laws of Moses and Israel."

They had become engaged.

This Love of Ours . . .

What was your engagement like? What's your story? Couples today often love to share their engagement story with friends and family. They detail fun, creative, and sometimes elaborate plans after the fact and post them on their wedding website for families and guests to enjoy.

Can you recall your engagement story? How much planning went into it? Who was involved? At what point in the development of your relationship did you decide to become engaged? Who, along with you, was in on the plan? Are both of your versions of the story the same? How are your stories the same or different? Did it play out the way you had intended? If you could do it all over again, what would you do the same? What would you do different?

If Jake and Abby were leaning toward the creative side of things, Charlie and Anna were certainly situated on the logical, sequential, purposeful, no-nonsense, and practical side of things. When Charlie proposed to Anna, she was about as surprised as Abby was when Jake proposed, but not because a dog was in the picture. To her, Charlie's proposal just seemed to come so fast.

"We hadn't known each other for that long," she told me. "And we hadn't even met each other's families. Charlie caught me a little off guard, that's all. So I told him that I needed some time to think about it!"

Anna would be the first to admit she was really "old school" about all this. For Anna, the timing was more about having the opportunity to meet each other's families. For Charlie, the timing had everything to do with a sale that was going on at a local jewelry store.

"I asked Charlie if he thought we should meet each other's families first," Anna continued. "But being a little on the—shall we say—'tight side' with money, and knowing the jewelry sale was limited to just a few days, he just couldn't hold himself back. So he bought me a ring before we'd met any of each other's families."

Ring or no ring, it was important for Anna that Charlie meet her family. So she decided it would be best to invite everyone to her home for dinner so they could meet the man who was captivating her heart.

"So, Anna," I said, "that must have been a bit nerve-wracking to have to get your house in order for a gathering like that, not to mention preparing a meal on top of everything else!"

"Yes," she said. "It was a pretty special time, that's for sure."

I was curious about a dinner that included an introduction of her future fiancé and husband to her family. So I leaned forward on the table and asked, "Anna, what on earth do you serve at a dinner party like that?"

She looked at me with a kind of "Mona Lisa" smile and simply replied,

"Meatloaf."

As it turned out, it was a fabulous evening. Anna's family embraced Charlie as one of their own. With that, Charlie passed inspection, and the date for their wedding was set.

Charlie and Anna would often look back to that evening as another significant part of the movement in their marriage. They would come to share many meals together. They would also come to share the company of an Unseen Guest, who would deepen the treasure of sharing not only that table and those meals together but also life beyond that table, beyond those meals, that would prove to be bonding in ways no one could anticipate.

5

Invitation

*"Affection is responsible for nine-tenths of whatever solid
and durable happiness there is in our natural lives."*

—C.S. Lewis, *The Four Loves*

At 6:22 in the morning, as the first rays of light began to push
back against the inky darkness of the previous night, no one
could have possibly comprehended the significance the day
ahead would hold. Make no mistake, so much more than just
another new day was dawning. Much more than just the darkness of the previous night was being dispelled. Much more than
the German countryside was being illuminated that day.

It was the thirtieth of September, the last Thursday of the
month. The year was 1452. A former stonecutter and goldsmith
by the name of Johannes Gutenberg, living in the German city
of Mainz, had just literally cranked out the first printed pages
of what we now know as the Gutenberg Bible. A year before, he
had invented a printing press system that used moveable type,
now known as the Gutenberg Press. This invention set into
motion a reformation of such biblical proportions that not only
would the narrative of human history be changed forever but
also the way that story was told. The invention that fueled the

Reformation would also impact what would become the wedding industry all these years later.

Before the invention of Gutenberg's press, a bellman or "town crier" verbally announced invitations to weddings. Typically, this person was an officer in the royal court who routinely made announcements in the community by walking through the streets and broadcasting in a loud voice the news of the day. It was understood that anyone hearing the proclamation was invited to the celebration.

During the Middle Ages, it was a common practice for the upper class, the nobility, to send written invitations. Families who could pay for such services would often hire monks who had been trained in calligraphy to create custom, handcrafted invitations that included a small piece of tissue to prevent the ink from smudging. These invitations were often double-enveloped as a way of protecting them from the wear and tear that often occurred during the transportation—usually on horseback.

Over the course of generations, these methods of inviting gave way to higher quality invitations, as well as the ability to mass-produce them. The spoken voice gave way to calligraphy, calligraphy gave way to engraving, and engraving gave way to lithography and then thermography—a process in which a plastic dust was applied to wet ink and heated to create the appearance of embossing. Today, laser engraving is used on all kinds of surfaces, including wood, metal, glass, and stone, making the art of invitation even more specialized.

Of course, none of this was on Jake or Abby's mind when they began to think about their own invitations. But given the countless ways that invitations have been given and received through the centuries, it was not that unusual for Jake to arrange for his invitation to Abby to be delivered by an animal of the canine variety. And as cautious as they were about their request to have their springer spaniel deliver the rings in the wedding ceremony, how much more time and thought they put into the deeper question—the question nearly every bride and groom wrestles with at one point or another: "Who will we invite to our wedding?"

We can be certain that when the couple in Cana of Galilee got ready for that festive wedding on that joyous afternoon two millennia ago, the invitations were sent the old-fashioned way: verbally. And it's safe to say that word of mouth traveled quickly and spread far and wide. There is also a strong indication, given the amount of wine set aside for this weeklong party—nearly 180 gallons, which, if you do the math, works out to roughly around 2800 glasses of wine—that this young couple had quite a community around them and expected most to join them. This was a couple who knew the power of community. Their family and friends had been there through the years, were with them on this day, and would continue to be with them, willing to add their blessing to that day and all the days that followed.

It would be fascinating to speculate about the details of this particular biblical narrative, and we might find it interesting to ask all manner of questions about the wedding. What kind of day was it? Did all the decorations arrive in good condition? Was the *chuppah* staked out securely in case sudden winds came up? Were the musicians rehearsed and ready—or were there any musicians at all? We might wonder if the flower girl and the ring bearer were really capable of walking down the dusty aisle (if there was an aisle), and who was going to tend to them during the ceremony, or even if there was a flower girl or a ring bearer at all.

We might be curious as to whether the mother of the groom was feeling honored or overlooked, or if the father of the bride was holding it all together. Some might find it interesting to know why Mary is referred to only as the "mother of Jesus" and not simply as "Mary" in John's account, or what her connection to these families might have been. And then, of course, we can only wonder about the role Jesus might have played in the lives of the family members up to this point. It might even be intriguing to learn who among the disciples knew the bride, the groom, or their families, or even why John doesn't provide the couple's names in such a remarkably important story.

But, in the end, none of that matters because the story really isn't about the weather, or the venue of the wedding, or the musicians, or the bridesmaids, or the groomsmen. It's not about the parents of the couple or even the couple themselves. The story isn't about any of that. The story is about Jesus and the invitation the couple gave him.

On the surface, this is a story about Jesus being invited to the wedding. And while that may be important, on a much deeper and far more profound level, this is a story about the couple inviting Jesus to the marriage. What matters most is that we understand the difference between them inviting Jesus to the wedding and inviting Jesus to the marriage.

Any teacher of linguistics or professor of etymology will tell you the hard work of learning another language has a huge payoff when the student begins to understand not just the words but also the nuances and the deeper shades of meaning that come with understanding a different language. With the help of historical data and the capacity to read between the lines, we discover the writer of this ancient story is telling us a great deal more than what we merely read on the page.

According to the Wycliffe Bible translators, the complete Bible has been translated into more than 500 languages, and many, if not most, of those languages use the word "wedding" to describe the event that took place in Cana of Galilee. In nearly all the current and common translations, as well as the paraphrases of this ancient story, we learn that along with Mary and the disciples, Jesus was also invited to the wedding. That is the prevailing sense—that Jesus was invited to the wedding.

As John conveys the guest list for the reader, he writes this: "Jesus and his disciples had also been invited to the *wedding*" (John 2:2, emphasis added). But there is more here than what meets the eye. Much more. While paraphrasers and translators most often prefer the word "wedding" to indicate the event to which the guests had been invited, the meaning intended by John in the original language is much different, and the implications are much deeper. John's message is clear: Jesus and his disciples had also been invited to the *marriage*.

Jesus and his disciples were invited not merely to attend the festivities taking place on a particular day at a particular time in a particular place. The couple in Cana had invited Jesus into their community of friends and family. They had invited him to walk deeply into their commitment with them and provide what only an invited and committed community can provide on every day, at every time, and in every place. To say that Jesus was invited to the *wedding* communicates a simple fact. To say that Jesus was invited to the *marriage* communicates a profound truth. It is something entirely different.

Charlie and Anna were up for something entirely different as well. As I talked with them about the spiritual development of their life together, it revealed their intentional connection with John's choice of words. We talked about how their wedding would indeed happen on a particular day at a particular time in a particular place with a particular gathering of people. But Charlie and Anna also shared the long view of that into which they were entering. They knew their marriage would be something more, something well beyond time and place, and would mature through years of their growing commitment to each other along with their constant, ongoing invitation to Jesus to be in their marriage.

So Charlie and Anna asked the all-important question: "Who will we invite to our wedding?" Together, they created their list. In fact, they made several lists, first on napkins and the backs of old receipts, and then in notebooks. In keeping with current custom, their wedding invitations were sent out eight weeks in advance to the friends and family members they desired to surround them on their wedding day. They followed these invitations with that previously mentioned, time-tested, well-trusted, centuries-old method: "word of mouth."

Charlie and Anna registered with an Internet wedding site. They invited their friends and family to not only simply watch their wedding plans unfold online but also actively participate with them by entering into their story—to learn about where they met, who introduced them, where they went on their first date, how they became engaged, who would be a part of their wedding party, where Charlie and Anna would spend their honeymoon, and their new address after the wedding.

These invitations were far more than mere announcements, proclamations, and communication of information. With each invitation to the wedding, Charlie and Anna were communicating two other important messages. First, they were expressing their deep sense of gratitude to each person for sharing the commitment to "walk deeply" with them through thin spaces of bane as well as the thick days of blessing they had known—and would know—in their life together. The invitations carried deep expressions of gratitude to each person for his or her commitment to the relationship. Second, each invitation carried the hope and expectation that each family member and friend who would join them on their wedding day—a brief moment in time—would also continue to join them in their marriage journey.

This Love of Ours . . .

If you've ever been in on planning a wedding, you know how important, if not difficult, it can be to create the guest list. If you haven't had your wedding yet and are still in the planning process, take some time to talk about whom you will invite. Also talk about the assumptions you have about who will be invited. Specifically, what criteria are you using to make the list? Are you feeling pressured from family members to invite certain people, or, conversely, to not include some individuals? How has this chapter helped you think differently about your invitation list? Consider together what it would mean to invite Jesus to your wedding. How does that find expression—or not—in your ceremony?

If you've already celebrated a wedding, look back on your guest list. If you had it to do over again today, how would it look the same or different? Who would you invite? Who might not make the list? Why? If you've invited Christ to your marriage, what does that look like for the two of you? Specifically, you might want to explore a book together that supports spiritual growth in relationship. (Drs. Les and Leslie Parrott, leading marriage enrichment specialists from the Seattle area, offer tremendous resources for couples who not only want to grow together relationally but also want to explore the spiritual dimension of their life together. You can find many great resources for your relationship at http://www.lesandleslie.com.)

There was no doubt in my mind that it would be a beautiful wedding day for Charlie and Anna. But they were inviting their families and friends to move beyond simply watching them get married; beyond merely spectating and passively witnessing;

beyond simply watching and listening to them speak their vows to each other. On their wedding day, Charlie and Anna were inviting their community of friends and family to consider the deeper beauty and significance of inviting Jesus into a marriage. They were inviting them to consider inviting Jesus into the very crucible of an ongoing journey of trust, commitment, engagement, and invitation into the movement toward love.

Sometime later, as I stood at my mailbox and held the invitation to Charlie and Anna's wedding, I began to have an inkling of how inviting Jesus to their marriage—not merely to their wedding—would make all the difference. It would make all the difference in times to come when the celebrations couldn't get any richer and the challenges couldn't get any more difficult.

6

Ceremony

"To get the full value of joy you must have someone to divide it with."

—Mark Twain, *Following the Equator*

So much has changed in the wedding industry during the past several decades. A quick Google search of "unique wedding venues" reveals what we probably already know: when it comes to unique places to celebrate a wedding, the more unique the better. Today, couples celebrate their union in special places from chapels to butterfly habitats, wineries to waterfront settings, country clubs to city halls, museums to historical venues, and city parks to botanical gardens. What we might have described as a traditional church wedding a generation ago can look very different today. Couples who may be cautious of musty old churches and stuffy sanctuaries without air conditioning in the middle of July can now choose to tie the knot in subzero temperatures in any number of ice bars across Europe. But that's only the tip of the iceberg.

Weddings take place at all times of day and night and in many different locations—land, sea, and sky. Consider these creative, if not alternative, ceremonies. One couple gathered their family and friends into the place where they met: a

McDonalds in Dayton, Ohio. Another couple, diving enthusiasts, hired a diving company with access to coral reefs and their own officiants to conduct their underwater ceremony. A young bride and groom, who met while working for an advertising company, were married "somewhere around 35,000 feet" in Virgin Airline's first-ever flight to Las Vegas. The guests were ushered in and seated on either "the bride's side" or "the groom's side" of the aircraft while billionaire Virgin Records tycoon Sir Richard Branson officiated. The bride and groom walked down the "aisle" of the aircraft to the song "Love Is in the Air." And because the sky is apparently not the limit, Branson is making plans to conduct a wedding ceremony some seventy miles above the earth—in space.

For more than three decades, I've enjoyed participating in unique "offsite" weddings. One took place on the spectacular shores of Lake Superior on an early summer morning. There were fewer than a dozen people in attendance, all dressed in blue jeans, T-shirts, and sandals. Another took place in the vast outdoor acreage of a botanical garden. More than a dozen attendants stood on either side of the bride and groom, wearing ground-length gowns and black tuxedoes with tails, as hundreds of guests looked on. But what remains far-and-away (no pun intended) the most unique ceremony over which I've presided was for a bride who stood with me in my office, along with her maid of honor, while the groom stood with his best man in a military chaplain's office more than 4,000 miles away on an army base in Germany. That certainly brought new meaning to the phrase "long-distance romance"!

Whether it's inside or outside, large or small, casual or formal, the venue of a wedding ceremony, the size of the gathering, and what people in those wedding parties are wearing has little to do with the lasting quality of a marriage. It is, as they say, "what's on the inside that counts."

Charlie and Anna had talked about "what's on the inside" and how it counted for them. They had experienced enough in their lives to warrant such awareness. But that wasn't to say Charlie didn't have a sense of excitement and anticipation for how Anna would look as she came down the aisle on their wedding day. At one point, Charlie turned to me and with a twinkle in his eye said, "You should see the dress that Anna is going to wear on our wedding day." But both of them knew their wedding day wasn't merely about a dress. Or a tux.

That's precisely what the apostle Paul was getting at in his letter to the Colossians. He urged Christ followers to be clothed with the things that do not go back to a rental agency, or wind up in a closet for decades, or are recycled for Halloween costumes, or—worst of all—get repurposed into curtains. Paul encouraged Christ followers in every age and in every time "to put on" and "be clothed with" "be clothed with" things like compassion, kindness, humility, meekness, patience, forgiveness, love, and harmony. These are things that have a far longer shelf-life than mere clothing. They make up the fabric of daily life in community. They are the garments of healthy, sustainable, life-giving relationships. They are the things that will not wear out or go out of style.

In another letter, this one to the church in Philippi, Paul reached out to a community of followers with a veritable wardrobe of essentials by urging his friends to keep focused on whatever is true, honorable, just, pure, pleasing, commendable, excellent, and praiseworthy. I've consistently said that in any of our relationships, if we held fast to these eight characteristics, the world would be a different place.

Through the years, mostly on or at least near our wedding anniversary, Nancy Lee and I have retrieved our wedding album and taken another walk through ever-increasingly distant memories. Once we've gotten past the large glasses, big hair, and wide lapels (and that's just me), we've been able to focus on more important things. For instance, we've focused on the people around us who modeled compassion and taught us kindness. We've recalled the people in our lives who exemplified humility. We've reflected on how that has fostered patience in our lives. We've talked about how those old photographs remind us of the importance of patience and the power of practicing forgiveness in our own marriage. We've reflected on the discipline of practicing whatever is true, honorable, just, pure, pleasing, commendable, excellent, and praiseworthy, and how doing so adds strength to the foundation of our relationship. All of that, of course, helps us renew our commitment to growing in love, living in harmony together, and passing that on to our own children and grandchildren.

Healthy relationships grow out of a commitment to constant attention to detail. For at least two millennia, these words of Paul have echoed into and through the lives of people desiring deeper connection with one another.

This Love of Ours . . .

Spend some time together talking about details. If you've already celebrated a wedding, recall the ceremony. What did you wear? What were the decorations like? What process did you go through to arrive at your decisions? How much time did you commit to planning the details of the final plan? How did things look on the outside? If you had to do it all over again, what would remain the same? What would you change?

If you're still in the planning stages, how do the apostle Paul's words influence the planning yet to do? Considering the amount of time and attention that go into planning a wedding ceremony and the subsequent reception (what to wear, who is invited, how the venue will be decorated), how much time and energy will you put into nurturing your relationship on a daily basis? Knowing what you know now about putting on and clothing yourselves with things that will last, how does that challenge you to live together differently?

Specifically, what are you doing to live more compassionately and with more kindness? Where in your relationship can you live with more humility and compassion? In what specific ways can you show more kindness, humility, and meekness? What would you have to change to show more patience and forgiveness to create more love and harmony? Finally, as you respond to Paul's invitation to think about an essential wardrobe, how can you intentionally focus on whatever is true, honorable, just, pure, pleasing, commendable, excellent, and praiseworthy in your relationship? Which of these need nurturing? Which of these are already in place?

As the ceremony began on the day of Charlie and Anna's wedding, I stood with Charlie near the altar, waiting for Anna to appear at the other end of the aisle. I thought back to that moment some months before when Charlie turned to me and with a twinkle in his eye said, "You should see the dress that Anna is going to wear on our wedding day." When Anna finally made her way down the aisle toward her waiting groom, Charlie turned to me and smiled. I winked back. At just that moment, the photographer snapped another photograph. It was an image that found its way into an album that, some years later, would capture more than words could possibly say. But we would try.

It was indeed a wedding to remember. But far more than just a formality, it was an expression of Charlie and Anna's deep commitment to walk boldly into the crucible of marriage together, come what may. And it may come as no surprise that in the midst of the celebrations that couldn't get any richer and the challenges that couldn't get any more difficult, for Charlie and Anna it was truly what was on the inside that counted the most—the desire to live with more compassion, kindness, humility, meekness, patience, forgiveness, love, and harmony. These were things that would endure beyond a wedding ceremony; things that would sustain a marriage. While certain things would not remain as they had once been, they would endure in other ways.

From the first century, the apostle Paul provided some enduring encouragement for any twenty-first-century couple who wonder what might lie beyond their ceremony:

> So we're not giving up. How could we! Even though on the outside it often looks like things are falling apart on us, on the inside, where God is making new life, not a day goes by without his unfolding grace. These hard times are small potatoes compared to the coming good times, the lavish celebration prepared for us. There's far more here than meets the eye. The things we see now are here today, gone tomorrow. But the things we can't see now will last forever (2 Corinthians 4:16–18 MSG).

Section Three

Crucible

When the wine gave out, the mother of Jesus said to him,
"They have no wine."

John 2:3

7

Marriage

"Marriage is not a noun; it's a verb. It isn't something you get. It's something you do. It's the way you love your partner every day."

—Barbara De Angelis

As I mentioned, Nancy Lee and I celebrated our wedding in the oil-boom town of Williston, North Dakota, on a hot, dry, dusty Saturday evening in July 1982. Friends and family gathered with us in the air-conditioned sanctuary of Our Redeemer's Lutheran Church from such distant points as Seattle, Oak Harbor, and Bellingham, Washington, as well as Santa Rosa, California, and Minneapolis, Minnesota. It was an evening ceremony that featured just about everything one might expect at a wedding: a festive procession, hymns, readings, a sermon, a couple of original pieces of music, communion, and an even more festive recessional.

We even had a pastor who wept as we exchanged our vows. I thought I might cry as well, but as soon as I saw the pastor weeping, I said to myself, *Gauche, get a grip; not right here and not right now! You can cry later!* Which I did. (More on that in a moment.) Yet, as if all that wasn't profound enough, what happened in the next moment is something I've wondered about for years. In that brief moment just after Nancy Lee and I had spoken our vows to each other, and right before my best man began singing an original song he'd written for our wedding, I looked into Nancy Lee's sweet face. As I held her soft hands in mine, I spoke softly but with nearly uncontainable joy, "We're married! We're really married!"

But I have to confess I've always wondered about what I said just then. Were we *really* married just then, at that very moment? And if so, how did that happen? Was it something someone said, or did, or thought? Was it in that very moment when we spoke our promises to each other? Or was it when the first measures of the processional music began to fill that fragrant candle-lit sanctuary? Was it during the reading of the Scriptures, or was it during the communion service as we all shared bread and wine? Was it when we made the trip to the courthouse to pick up the wedding license, or was it when the witnesses signed it?

I will be the first to acknowledge the pervasive mystery of God in all of this, but still, I wanted to know when and at what point we were actually married. Is there really a moment? Or could it be that marriage is something that defies a point, an event, on a linear line? Could it be that marriage is what comes of all these moments and happens as a result of them?

Most of Charlie and Anna's family and friends had been seated. We were just minutes away from the beginning of the ceremony. The wedding party was waiting just outside the chapel for their cue to enter. As I stood at the front of the chapel and looked out on the gathering of guests, I was able to take in the whole scene at once. The candles were flickering gently around the room. A large arrangement of beautiful roses lay just to one side of the reading table. The guitarist was gently playing the prelude. Charlie and Anna's family and friends were settling in and eagerly waiting. Finally, the small clock on the back wall indicated the time had come. The moment was at hand.

A brief moment of silence was followed by a familiar melody from the musician on her guitar. Conversations between guests and family members quieted, and they turned to see the best man and the maid of honor enter the room. Slowly and deliberately, they made their way to their places near the altar at the front of the chapel, and then turned and waited. The guests once again turned their attention toward the entrance. As I invited the guests to stand, Charlie and Anna stepped into the room together. It was an extraordinary moment for them—not only stepping across the physical threshold of the entrance into the chapel, but more remarkable still, stepping across an invisible threshold into a completely new place in their lives together. They were, in a very real sense, taking steps from a physical place in a room in a building among friends and family into a deeper reality—a wider, broader kind of spiritual place in their lives together without structure, borders, walls, or any other kind of barrier or hindrance.

The time had come. The moment was at hand. As I watched them walk into the chapel, the thought occurred to me that all this had not just started for Charlie and Anna; it had already begun a long, long time ago. Their wedding ceremony was certainly just starting, but their marriage had already begun—or, more precisely, was already taking place. For Charlie and Anna, the time they had planned for had finally come. But in that one moment of chronological time, something had shifted. The chronological time, which had been ticking away until just a few moments ago, seemed to stop. This chronological time, or *chronos* time, measured in hours, minutes, and even seconds, had ceased. In that one instant we were suddenly in between time. We were in *kairos* time.

The time had come. The moment was at hand. The hands on the clock became irrelevant as this moment-in-between-moments seemed to slow and somehow widen. I watched as Charlie and Anna made their way down the aisle to the place they would promise their love to each other, seek the blessing of their friends and families, and ask for God's blessing on their lives together. The chronological moment they had dreamed of, planned for, and talked about for so long had suddenly become a timeless moment of deep, immeasurable, and nearly uncontainable joy. For Charlie and Anna, the timelessness of *kairos* was at hand.

This date on a calendar, this time on a clock, this moment that for so long had been penciled into a planner, tracked on a timeline, and might even have been managed with a smartphone app and calculated in a spreadsheet, was now fully upon them. And they were fully alive to its significance. Side by side, hand in hand, step by step, Charlie and Anna walked into the chapel to celebrate not just their wedding but also their marriage. In that moment, they knew they had each other. In that moment, they knew God had them. In that moment-in-between-moments, they knew—perhaps more than they had ever known before—that was enough. That was just enough.

At the altar, Anna stood close to Charlie, at his left side. In her left hand she held a bouquet of flowers, and with her right hand she held tightly to Charlie's arm. As the music ended, they looked at each other, smiled, and then looked back at me. Charlie and Anna had both waited a lifetime to embrace this moment—this one, poignant moment. As they stood together in the midst of their family and friends, what seemed most powerful was their deeply held trust that God was present with them in this moment. God was with them now, just as God had been present with them in every moment, through all of life's moments of love, laughter, pain, and healing, as they charted their way through life, death, and now, once again, new life.

The time had come. The moment was at hand. This moment—this one bright, shining moment-in-between-moments, was what they had dreamed about, talked about, planned for, and were now living into fully. The ceremony was beginning. But one could only wonder when all of it really began and, more importantly, *when* were they married.

On the morning I met Nancy Lee Johnson on the top step of Stub Hall, we spent five, maybe ten, minutes talking and laughing together. In the minutes that followed our parting on that sunny morning, I said to my friend Bill as we walked down the hall to our rooms, "I'm going to marry that girl!" There was a deep sense of resolve in my heart at that moment that never wavered. Four months later, on Nancy Lee's birthday, we were engaged. Six months after that, we celebrated a wedding. Yet the question remains: *When were we married?*

In the same way we asked when commitment begins, we wondered when, along the course of the days, weeks, and months that followed our meeting in September, our marriage began. Was it when we first met? Was it when Nancy Lee tripped and fell into my arms? Was it during our first few conversations or between classes on the way to the library? Was it after our first tears, or before our first argument, or at some point during our first date? Was it after our first, second, or third experience of unbridled laughter, when we began to feel fully alive with one another and completely safe and unreserved in each other's presence?

Was it weeks earlier when we made the trip to the courthouse to pick up the wedding license, or was it when the witnesses signed it? Was it during the first measures of the processional as the music began to fill that fragrant, candle-lit sanctuary? Or was it during the reading of the Scriptures? Was it in that very moment when we voiced our promises to each other or during communion as we all shared bread and wine, or in the most intimate moments, days, weeks, months after the wedding? When? When were we married?

To use an agrarian metaphor, marriage is like a seed that is planted in the ground and watered. It begins to grow, even if imperceptibly, until it finally emerges into daylight. It's like asking, "When is a plant a plant?" Is the plant only a plant when it germinates? Is the plant a plant when it pushes through the soil into daylight? Or is the plant the plant inside that seed before it is put into the ground? In the same way, it could be said there exists a particular moment in chronological time when a marriage "sparks" and begins to take shape and grow. This all happens in quiet, remote, even intimate and hidden places in human hearts when a couple arrives at that proverbial "fork in the road" and choose to take it together.

Such was the case centuries ago for that young couple in Cana of Galilee. By the time their wedding day finally arrived, and they stood together under the *chuppah* with the rabbi in front of them and their family and friends behind them, they were, in a sense, already (but not yet) quite married. There was also for them, as well, a kind of *kairos* moment emerging in their life together. There was an "already/not yet" character to the commitment they had made with one another. The two of them were already living into the hope and promise of faithfulness and trust, but the fruit of that faithfulness could not yet be completely known. They were already living into the promise to honor, serve, and care for each other, but the blessings of their sacrifice could not yet be fully counted. They were already living into the hope and expectation that the promises they made on their (*chronos*) wedding day would translate into daily (*kairos*) marriage commitments to live in love and forgiveness until the end of their lives. Yet the significance of such a spectacular marriage together could not yet be fully grasped.

The reality of marriage is oftentimes less than spectacular. Charlie and Anna would come to know that. There would be days ahead that would end in spectacular ruin. There would be weeks, perhaps even months, ahead that would seem utterly and spectacularly desolate. Far from the splendor of that one bright, shining day, Charlie and Anna would trade their wedding garments for sackcloth and ashes. They would begin to wonder if the God who had blessed them with this day had abandoned them on other days. They would wonder if God's promises could be trusted. They would struggle with hope.

But for now, the time had come for Charlie and Anna, and the moment was at hand. Their wedding day had arrived, and so had their marriage. This moment—this one, bright, shining moment-in-between-moments—had fully arrived, and with it came the good news that the promise once spoken under a *chuppah* in Cana was being spoken once again. The promise once made to that couple in Cana was being made once again to this couple in this sanctuary. Like cool, refreshing water being poured into stone water jars and filled to the brim, the good news of God's faithfulness was being poured into Charlie and Anna's life together.

God's promise of abundance in the face of scarcity would continue to manifest itself in Charlie and Anna's life. God would refresh the parched terrain of their marriage and cause it to flourish once again. For now, Charlie and Anna would live in hope, knowing and believing the fulfillment of God's promises was already a present reality, though not yet fully revealed. They would live in the hope and promise that God's word once spoken under a *chuppah* in Cana was being spoken now in this place and time. For now, Charlie and Anna would continue to live in the hope present in this one moment, on this one particular day, at this particular time, in this particular place—a place where they were witnessing the fulfillment of God's promise to them.

On their wedding day, Charlie and Anna celebrated the promise that their hope would constantly be translated into faith in things yet unseen. And when it comes to God's promises, Charlie and Anna would be people who would dare to believe that even when nothing seems to have changed, everything has indeed changed. That would be the promise that carried them through uncertainty and the unknown into the years of their marriage.

This Love of Ours . . .

Perhaps this chapter has gotten you thinking. The difference between *chronos* and *kairos* time can be easily lost in our fast-paced lives. If we don't allow ourselves a slower pace and time to consider these more timeless moments, we run the risk of missing them all together. So take some time and consider the question, "When were you married?" Can you pinpoint a time (*chronos*), or has marriage taken place over time (*kairos*)? What went into the decision to either ask your partner or to say yes?

Talk with each other about some of the more significant bonding moments you've experienced in your marriage and explore how those moments add up to a more significant and ongoing marriage. How has your commitment to building your marriage helped and equipped you to press on with trust and faith into the future that cannot be seen? As you think about these things and the future ahead of you, consider the words to this prayer. You may wish to use them to inform your own prayer as you continue to build your marriage.

Lord God, you have called your servants to adventures of which we cannot see the ending, by paths as yet untrodden, through perils unknown. Give us faith to go out with good courage, not knowing where we go, but only that your hand is leading us and your love supporting us; through Jesus Christ our Lord. Amen.

As the candles flickered in the chapel, Katie, one of Anna's closest friends, stepped toward the lectern and opened her Bible. She turned to a story that still survives centuries upon centuries of telling and retelling. It was, of course, the recounting of an ordinary event with an extraordinary twist; a common tale of relationship with an uncommon turn of love. It was the reading from the Gospel of John, the second chapter . . . the wedding in Cana of Galilee.

> Three days later there was a wedding in the village of Cana in Galilee. Jesus' mother was there. Jesus and his disciples were guests also. When they started running low on wine at the wedding banquet, Jesus' mother told him, "They're just about out of wine."
>
> Jesus said, "Is that any of our business, Mother—yours or mine? This isn't my time. Don't push me."
>
> She went ahead anyway, telling the servants, "Whatever he tells you, do it."
>
> Six stoneware water pots were there, used by the Jews for ritual washings. Each held twenty to thirty gallons. Jesus ordered the servants, "Fill the pots with water." And they filled them to the brim.
>
> "Now fill your pitchers and take them to the host," Jesus said, and they did.

When the host tasted the water that had become wine (he didn't know what had just happened but the servants, of course, knew), he called out to the bridegroom, "Everybody I know begins with their finest wines and after the guests have had their fill brings in the cheap stuff. But you've saved the best till now!"

This act in Cana of Galilee was the first sign Jesus gave, the first glimpse of his glory. And his disciples believed in him. (John 2:1–11 MSG)

The words lingered in the air for a brief moment before Katie closed the Bible and stepped back to her seat. As the room quieted, and just before I began to share some thoughts on what we had just heard, Charlie and Anna each took a deep breath. It was one of those contented, relaxed, and profoundly grateful deep breaths. I looked at Charlie, and then at Anna, and softly whispered, "This is such a great moment. Don't you just love it?"

Anna looked at Charlie, smiled, tightened her grip on his arm, and softly replied, "I do."

8

Promises

*"Being with you is like walking on a very clear morning;
I definitely have the sensation of belonging there."*

—E.B. White

I'm pretty sure I know why our officiating pastor wept as Nancy Lee and I exchanged our vows. He was lost in the significance of the gathering of the young adults in the wedding party, most of whom he'd nurtured in the faith from the time they were in grade school. I was lost in the significance of trying to remember the vows that I'd memorized. I'd had them down cold, but for some reason I had suddenly forgotten them.

Nancy Lee and I wrote our own vows. A month before our wedding we wrote out a dozen drafts of the things we wanted to promise to each other. These were our non-negotiables—the values we were both bringing to the marriage. We knew we had to get this accomplished because the task of memorizing the vows would take some time. Starting the week before our wedding— a full seven days—Nancy Lee and I spoke our vows to each other, out loud, at least once a day. Doing this reassured both of us that when the time came time to say our vows during the ceremony itself, we'd be fully present and in the moment with each other, familiar with what we were saying, and equipped to speak those words with confidence.

On the day of our wedding, I handed the pastor the piece of paper on which I had written our vows and asked him to have them ready "just in case something happened." But I told him not to worry, because I had them memorized. "I've got these down cold," I said.

When we got to the moment in the ceremony where we exchanged vows, Nancy Lee handed her bouquet to her maid of honor and turned toward me. We took each other's hands, and then I took a deep breath and I began.

> *Nancy Lee, the journey toward becoming one with you is an adventure in faith, a celebration of new life, and a joy beyond anything I've ever known. You are a gift from God to me. And before God and in the presence of our families and friends gathered here to celebrate with us, I commit myself to you with these promises.*

All the rehearsing we had done—the daily repetition over and over again—was paying off perfectly! I continued,

> *I love you, and I want to share my life with you and be your husband. I promise you my love and faithfulness, my respect and commitment to serving you in love as Jesus has taught us to serve. I commit to you all that I am and promise to be your best friend in all our joys and sorrows, laughter and tears, as we seek to glorify our Lord.*

At some point in the middle of this section, I suddenly had a random thought. As I was speaking my vows—arguably the most important words I'd ever say to Nancy Lee—I discovered that I was, of all things, multitasking. I was saying these deeply

profound words of promise out loud to Nancy Lee in a sanctuary filled with family, friends, and honored guests, but at the
same time I was asking myself one very important question:
What would happen if I suddenly forgot the next line?

All I can say is that I found out exactly what would happen.
After what seemed like an eternity in that moment, I turned
to the pastor who, I was sure, was carefully tracking with me.
Wasn't he? Of course he would be following along, silently reading the promises I had written on the piece of paper just in case
this very thing happened. Of course he would be anticipating
my gaffe and be ready to prompt me with the next word in the
next split second. Wouldn't he? Sure, he would have, except that
he couldn't because he was weeping. He would have, except that
he didn't know where he was, let alone where I was. Mercifully,
that moment passed in mere seconds, and I was able to regain
my place and continue on to the end.

*As your husband, and with God's help, I commit myself
to being your needs fulfilled as we share in the fullness
of life together. I take you with great joy to be my wife!*

Nancy Lee was next, and, true to form, she breezed through
her vows with poise, grace, beauty, and depth of feeling. For
every one of the thirty-four wedding anniversaries we've celebrated since, we've known this to be true: vows are the most
important words you'll ever speak to your lover. My dear friends
Cara and Mike know that.

I had known Cara for eight years when she and Mike
became engaged. To say I was thrilled for them would be an
understatement. If any couple was blessed not merely to be
blessed, but blessed to be a blessing to others, Cara and Mike
were that couple. They were passionate about life, committed

to their families, fiercely loyal when it came to friendships, and invested in serving others. They just had a way of drawing others into their sphere and showing grace and love. I was blessed beyond measure to call them friends and richly honored to have been invited to officiate at their wedding.

As the three of us sat together exploring their wedding plans over cups of coffee, Mike mentioned that his parents had given them "the most unique wedding present ever." When I asked what it was, Mike shared this story with me.

When Mike's parents, Jan and Tom, celebrated their wedding on Friday evening, June 7, 1974, at Trinity Lutheran Church in Long Lake, Minnesota, they faced each other, took each other's hands, and spoke their promises to one other. It was as profound a moment as they had ever experienced. Somehow they knew early on that if their vows were important enough to say in the company of friends and family on their wedding day, they were important enough to say often, even regularly. So Jan and Tom made a commitment to repeat their wedding vows to each other once a week.

They would be out to dinner together on a weekend, and over hors d'oeuvres and their favorite wine, they would say their vows to each other. They would be on vacation and say their vows to each other by the pool. They would encounter the occasional circumstances when work would necessitate them being apart, and they would be on the phone saying their vows to each other. Wherever they were, whatever they were doing, Jan and Tom would pause long enough to honor the commitment they had made to say their vows to each other often. They were determined to live into the promise of doing this, knowing that the promise would pay off in the long run. And they've been at it for more than forty years.

On the evening Cara and Mike were engaged, Jan and Tom challenged them to do the same—to make a commitment to say their vows to each other once a week. So, Mike and Cara have been doing just that each week since their wedding on Saturday, October 2, 2010, at the Prince of Peace Lutheran Church in Burnsville, Minnesota. They've been out to dinner on a weekend, and over hors d'oeuvres and wine they have looked across the table and said their vows. They have been on vacation in Arizona and have said their vows by the pool. They've said their vows to each other in Napa County. They've renewed their promises in a fjord in Norway, on a beach in Hawaii, and during a bike trip through the Julia Pfeiffer Burns State Park in California. They have renewed their vows while celebrating their anniversary hunkered down in a cozy cabin in Pepin, Wisconsin. And yet, for all the remarkable places Cara and Mike have recalled those promises, they would be the first to tell you it doesn't matter where they are. All that matters is that they are together.

Not long ago, I invited Cara and Mike to share their story with a group of young couples with whom I was planning weddings and preparing for marriage. When they arrived, they brought with them a large bag containing the matted and framed copies of the vows they had said to each other on their wedding day. Their vows now hang on a wall in their home—a daily reminder of the weekly promise to a lifetime of commitment.

Mike greeted the group and related what it was like growing up to hear and watch his parents say their vows to each other. He described the moment he spoke his own vows to Cara at their wedding. He didn't have to look at the words anymore; he had them down cold. Then he stood facing Cara, with her hands in his, looked in her eyes, and began:

Cara, we have shared so much together, and I love you to my core. And today, in the presence of God, family, and friends, I commit myself to you and our marriage with these promises: I promise to laugh with you, be faithful to you, forgive you, and live forever to make you giggle. You are my best friend, and I want to grow old with you on our porch. Every sunset on that porch, I promise to love you as much as I do right now. I am proud to be your husband and take you as my wife. I feel so blessed to share God's journey with my best friend. That journey, and our journey as one, starts today!

Cara's face beamed with love and pride as Mike came to the last line of his well-spoken, well-lived vows. She brightened still more, and her smile was sweet and contagious in a room half-filled with young brides-to-be who would give anything to begin a tradition like this and who will, perhaps, consider the blessing of such a tradition. Next it was her turn. She looked at Mike, took a breath, and started.

Michael, you are my soul mate and my best buddy. And today, in the presence of God, family, and friends, I commit myself to you and our marriage with these promises. I offer you my solemn vow to be your faithful partner . . . to love, laugh, and celebrate with you. I promise to trust you, respect you, forgive you, and strengthen you. I vow to be patient with you and work as a team through both our failures and successes. In your times of need, I will be there to support and encourage you . . . to hold and comfort you—and, of course, give you lots of hugs and kisses. I promise to appreciate you and all the blessings we will share in our life together. I am proud to be your wife. And today, with great joy, I take you as my husband, now and forever!

The room was quiet. The five couples sat motionless. All of us were silently pondering what we had just experienced: two very public declarations of personal and powerful commitments from Mike and Cara. We lingered there a moment longer, as the importance of what had just happened held the room nearly breathless.

I asked Mike and Cara if it was ever a challenge to carry this out. Cara said there were times when they both could hardly wait to share their weekly ritual, but she admitted there were other times when it was "just a matter of getting it done." But, she added, "It's the promise we made to share these each week and live into them that keeps us going."

When someone asked if they had a certain time of day or night to do this, Cara said she had a weekly reminder scheduled on her smartphone for Sunday evenings. The alarm played the classic "Bridal Chorus" from Richard Wagner's 1850 opera *Lohengrin*. She added, "Sometimes I'm running out the door to work when it goes off, and we just get to stop and say our vows—and then we're on our way!"

This Love of Ours . . .

Revisit your vows "to have and to hold, for richer, for poorer." Can you remember what you promised? What do you recall from your wedding ceremony? What was it like to speak those promises to each other? Did you speak them yourself, or did the person presiding over your ceremony speak them and have you respond with "I do"?

I've often asked couples whose marriages are nearing twenty-five, thirty-five, and even forty years to recall the promises they made on their wedding day. This is often followed by nervous laughter and some shuffling of the feet. The amount of uneasiness always seems to be in direct proportion to the number of years that have passed since their wedding day. But it's not long before the couple makes a genuine attempt to recall those promises made long ago.

If you're near your anniversary, go back into the scrapbook, pull out the audio recording, dig out the notes of the ceremony, and see if you can put your hands on your vows. If you're months away from the next celebration, you've got some time to prepare. Plan to set aside some time on your anniversary to say your vows again. If the original version of your promises is long gone, this might be a great time to renew, recommit, or even rewrite some promises going forward. Imagine your partner's surprise when your retrieve "the most important words you've ever spoken to each other" and say them once again. What would it mean to the two of you to make a commitment to repeat your vows to each other more frequently? Perhaps you could do this every year, or each month, or even more regularly.

Cara and Mike have been at this weekly ritual together for nearly four years. No doubt, they will someday have a powerful legacy of promise to pass along to another generation of lovers. They'll also pass along what Charlie and Anna have come to know: that it's the promise itself that holds everything together when everything seems to be coming apart.

And things do indeed come apart.

9

Crisis

"Day by day and night by night we were together. All else has long been forgotten by me."

—Walt Whitman, *Leaves of Grass*

It's not a matter of *if* but *when* a crisis will come.

Imagine the guests as they gather for the reception. Excitement fills the air as they enter the beautiful ballroom. Old friends mingle, and new acquaintances converse. The DJ, sounding much like an announcer at a professional basketball game, is heralding the imminent arrival of the wedding party. This creates even more buzz as guests look on with anticipation. The couple is soon introduced and makes their grand entrance.

Everything is just perfect. The tables are decorated with linen tablecloths and folded napkins. Everything is in place; the flatware is polished, the stemware is spotless. Months earlier, the bride and groom had met with the caterer. Together they had talked through seemingly endless options and made important decisions about everything from the hors d'oeuvres to the desserts. This included the balance of colors, textures, aromas, and the presentation. It had all been carefully planned.

Everything is just perfect. The hors d'oeuvres are spectacular. The servers move through the crowd with platters that include, among other things, Prosciutto-wrapped warm-stuffed dates and Buffalo meatballs with caramelized onions and tomato cognac glace. As the guests take their seats and dinner is served, the conversations continue to flow. The guests anticipate the entrees—chicken marsala, beef bourguignon, or pistachio-crusted salmon. It's truly a remarkable moment. The mood on this beautiful evening is carefree and festive.

Everything is just perfect. It is clear to the guests that an enormous amount of planning has gone into this moment. Every detail—the lighting in the room, the decorations on the tables, the seating arrangement of the guests, the nametags at each place setting, the temperature of the air, the temperature of the food, the DJ's playlists, the custom introductions of the wedding party—has been thought through, planned, poured over, and rehearsed so many times that absolutely *nothing* could possibly go wrong.

Except that *something* is going to go horribly wrong.

On the morning of the wedding, the catering staff arrives and gathers in the kitchen to prepare for the reception. On one end of the kitchen, there is a deep sink often used for thawing sealed packages of frozen food. One of the sous-chefs has gone to the freezer and pulled the necessary items. He sets them in the deep sink and begins the slow, steady stream of cool water over the bags. This will slowly and gently thaw the several thousand dollars' worth of frozen seafood. This has been a reliable method for him—one that he has used many times in the past with perfect success.

But at some point during the timeline of that day, someone in the kitchen goes to the sink and uses the faucet. He moves the faucet to the adjacent sink to rinse his hands, a pan, a pot, a knife. When he finishes washing—in a split-second and without a second thought—he leaves the cold water off. This leaves a slow but deliberate stream of hot tap water flowing over the mostly thawed seafood.

No one knows how much time elapsed between the introduction of the hot water and the moment the crisis was discovered. But one thing is for sure: the hot water not only completely thawed the delicate seafood but also started a poaching process, which in due time rendered everything inedible. This is a *big* problem.

When the lead caterer approaches the sink and discovers the debacle, he unleashes several moments of unbridled anger against the kitchen staff. He flings bags of sealed and now-unusable seafood against the far kitchen wall, which end up in a pile on the floor. What was just a moment before a finely tuned and well-stocked kitchen, awash with the strains of classical music and the sounds of cooks at work, is now practically a crime scene.

Disbelief among the staff morphs into shock as verbs, nouns, and adjectives seldom used in this setting (and even more rarely mingled together in such a unique manner) fill the air. These are terrifying minutes. It is a moment of utter crisis—a problem of biblical proportions. Running out of food at a reception of any kind is a huge problem. Chefs anywhere will tell you this ranks as one of the most dreaded situations. It can be devastating to a chef's reputation and a business, to say nothing of the families gathered to celebrate a wedding.

Not much has changed in that regard since the wedding in Cana of Galilee some 2,000 years ago. There was nothing amiss at that wedding—until the wine ran out. That's probably why this story has endured the ages and comes to us today. The ancient Gospel writer John tells us the situation plainly and refuses to soften the edges. "When the wine gave out, the mother of Jesus said to him, 'They have no wine.' And Jesus said to her, 'Woman, what concern is that to you and to me? My hour has not yet come'" (John 2:3–4).

For the couple and their families in Cana, running out of wine was a nightmare. It is difficult to overstate the importance of serving wine in first-century Jewish culture. Wine was a symbol of blessing and a sign of relationship with one another and with the holy. To run out of wine was more than an indication of poor planning; it cast an unfavorable (if not harsh) reflection on the host. Wine was meant to inspire, comfort, and lend dignity and importance to an occasion. Running out of it was a *big* problem.

I've sat with dozens of couples through the years who have "run out" of what once was plentiful and abundant in their relationship. It's human nature to wait until it's almost "too late." Notice that at the wedding in Cana nothing was said about the wine until it was gone—"They have no wine." The call usually comes from the marriage partner who's finally had enough.

As a last resort, the couple musters just enough courage to reach out for help. They've run out of some of the things they celebrated most on their wedding day. Their once bright, vibrant, life-giving relationship that reflected the light of hope has become dulled, if not tarnished, with the ordinariness of each day. They have become overwhelmed by the common routines of daily life and bored with the predictability of their routines. They've simply run out of the things that once breathed oxygen into their daily life together.

This Love of Ours . . .

There is a good chance you've experienced some of this—every couple does at some point. And while no one likes to talk about the things that are lacking in a relationship, those conversations are necessary. One of the most helpful ways of getting at the difficult conversations is to regularly set aside some time to "clear the air," "get it out," and "lay it all on the table." You can do this by setting aside some time each month to talk about the things that have seemed to stall or even impede the growth of your marriage.

Scheduling this time in advance will allow each partner to bring consideration to the issues that need to be discussed. Doing this in advance will also allow the emotion in the heat of the moment to subside, if not disappear altogether. It's almost never a good idea to have these conversations when emotions are running high—and it's never a good idea to start them after 10:00 PM. So it can be helpful to agree to come back to the issues that are most pressing after each of you has had some time to bring perspective to the issues. The important thing is to agree together to finish the conversation. The temptation is always to set things aside and not return to them, but you then run the risk of failing to talk about the issues and "clear the air." This will never fill back to the brim those things that have run out in the first place.

How have you dealt with crisis in your relationship? When things don't run as smoothly has you had hoped, how do you react? Are you a "first responder," or do you need some time to process issues in your own mind before talking openly about them?

Running out of anything at a reception pales in comparison with the things we run out of in life. The one common denominator in every relationship is that at some point, there will be challenges. We will run out of all kinds of things in our relationships. Calamity, chaos, and catastrophe in varying degrees are part of every relationship. It's what we choose do at that moment that makes all the difference.

Section Four

Counsel

His mother said to the servants, "Do whatever he tells you."

John 2:5

10

Advice

"There is no more lovely, friendly and charming relation-
ship, communion or company than a good marriage."

—Martin Luther, *Table Talk*

Fast-forward to the summer of 2012. Friday morning was dawning. Night was slowly giving way as shadows danced through
the trees, bounced off the houses, and rolled across the lawns as
if retreating from the emerging light. And then, in one glorious
instant, the sun appeared, making its first appearance just above
the horizon. A brand new day.

Light began pouring into our kitchen, but we had no idea
what shadow would soon return to cover us and pull us back
into the darkness. It was about 8:30, and the first pot of coffee
was brewing when Nancy Lee's cell phone rang. Our daughter,
Sarah, was calling from Charlottesville, Virginia, where she and
Travis, her husband of three years, were settling into the new
community after recently moving there from Princeton, New
Jersey. Nancy Lee excused herself from the kitchen where we
were chatting with a friend over breakfast. When she walked
into the next room, I could still hear the tension in her voice.
Her cheery greeting to Sarah was followed by an abruptly awkward silence; that longer-than-normal gap in the usual rhythm

of conversation. Ten minutes later, my apprehensions were confirmed when Nancy Lee stepped back into the kitchen. The effects of the phone call were all over her face.

"What?" I asked.

She paused, and then said, "That was Sarah. Travis has testicular cancer."

There is nothing like the stunned silence that follows a moment like that and the way the brain attempts to process such information. Neither is there much to compare with the kind of slow-motion punch-in-the-gut that strikes just a few seconds later when the data and emotion collide and begin to catch up with real time. To be sure, not much after an announcement like that really makes any difference. Certainly not breakfast.

The rest of the day was a blur for us. To say it was difficult to focus would have been an understatement. Focus was nearly impossible. We couldn't even imagine what it was like for Sarah and Travis.

Nothing prepares you for a moment like that.

Without a doubt, on that warm, sunny, summer wedding day three years earlier, as Sarah and Travis stood at the altar speaking their vows to each other, "for better or worse, for richer or poorer, in sickness and health," cancer of any stripe was the last thing on their minds.

In the week that followed, we were on the phone with Sarah and Travis just about every day, asking questions for which there were no immediate answers. We were sharing information and comparing notes on what to do next as we walked deeper into the even bigger question: "What does this mean?"

There were many things we did not know. We didn't know how Travis would react or respond to the treatment. We didn't know if or when his hair would fall out. We didn't know how well he'd be able to maintain focus on his studies, his teaching, or his homework—not to mention his ability to just relax.

But there was also much that we did know. We knew that following surgery, Travis would be cancer free. We knew that after one round of chemotherapy—eight infusions of power- ful drugs along with an ongoing barrage of far more powerful prayer—Travis could live with ninety-six percent assurance the cancer would not return. Even more important, we knew the prognosis for testicular cancer was very good. The oncologist reminded Sarah of this the moment after the diagnosis, when she took Sarah's sweet yet terrified face in her hands and, look- ing her directly in the eyes, said, "You will not lose your hus- band." And last, but not least—more appropriately, first and foremost—we knew what Sarah and Travis knew: that we all had each other, that God had all of us, and that was enough.

In marriage it's easy to run out. We run out of all kinds of things: energy, time, fire, passion, creativity, courage, love, patience, desire, adventure, health, love. You name it, we run out of it. To run out of wine at a wedding during the first century was a calamitous affair. It was literally a misstep, a social disas- ter. With the success of the wedding celebration foreshadowing the marriage, it was critical that everything go well. Disgrace, humiliation, insult—all these and more—would be heaped on the family who was careless enough to allow this to happen.

Yet in the story of matrimonial misfortune at the wedding in Cana, nine words were spoken over two sentences that changed the trajectory of this and every other debacle of relational decline that has since followed. Just as no one knew how much time the seafood in the caterer's kitchen had sat defrosting in the deep sink, no one at the wedding on that otherwise beautiful day in Cana knew how much time had elapsed between the pour- ing of the last drop of wine and the need for another glass. Yet one thing is for sure: the first four words out of Mary's mouth stated the eventual condition of every relationship: "They have no wine."

Notice Mary did not say, "They are running out of wine." There was no anticipation; there was no hope there. There was no holding out that they could, on their own, or by their own effort or strength, somehow save the day. There was no illusion that the family could somehow pull it together by running into the back room or even down the street to get more. No, Jesus' mother announced the cold, hard fact: "They have no wine."

None. They had run out.

At this point, no one was thinking metaphorically. There was nothing here (yet) about how friendships, relationships, or marriages run out of what they need to keep vital. None of that. That would come with time. But on this particular day at this particular time in this particular place at this particular moment, they literally needed some wine. They needed a miracle.

This Love of Ours . . .

We've all got models; others after whom we pattern our lives and relationships. For some of us, these models are family members: a parent, grandparent, uncle, aunt, or a sibling. For others of us, these models are other married couples who have healthy, thriving relationships, and pattering our own relationships and marriages after them is helpful. These are often the people to whom we go for advice.

Who might that be for you? Who is the person to whom you go for wisdom when things get complicated? Is there another couple in your life whose marriage is worth emulating? When things get a little chaotic in your own life and relationship, are you more likely to keep it to yourself, or do you have someone to whom you can go for help? As Mary's words echo through the centuries, right into your life today, to whom can you go when you hear the words, "Do whatever he tells you"?

In marriages—indeed, in every relationship anywhere—it's never a matter of what to do *if* the wine runs out but *when* the wine runs out. It's going to happen—the wine, the sparkle, the shine, the excitement of the relationship—is going to run out.

In our marriages, the list of things that we run out of is nearly endless. We run out of joy. We run out of faith. We run out of serving. We run out of respect. We run out of promises, celebration, and commitment. We run out of contentment, compassion, and kindness. We run out of humility, meekness, patience, forgiveness, love, laughter, and sorrow. We run out of health, tears, love, and life. Sometimes we just run out. We run the risk of running out of wine all the time.

It's at those very moments that the first-century words of Jesus' mother echo forward through the centuries into our twenty-first century experience: "Do whatever he tells you!"

But how do we do that? I imagine the advice of Jesus' mother must certainly have stopped the servants in their tracks. Their momentary silence wasn't so much out of reverence but out of disbelief. In that moment, they just stopped and were silent. That's good advice when we've run out.

It's ironic the number of voices today that remind us there's simply not enough silence in our lives. Certainly, with all the noise it's difficult, if not impossible, to listen well. On top of finding time to sit together as a couple and have deep conversations about the things that have drained out of the bottom of our relationship buckets is the challenge of finding time to simply sit and be still. Or, more precisely, *making* the time to sit and be still.

To do this, you must make an attempt. Commit some moments this week to sit and be still. Five minutes . . . ten minutes . . . perhaps push it to fifteen minutes, and clear your mind of pressing issues. This will be difficult at first, but the more time and space you make for silence, the better you will be able to listen. You may need to close your eyes and focus on a particular phrase or thought—the simpler the better. Perhaps pairing this with quiet breathing will help.

Try this: while breathing in, simply say to yourself, "Jesus, I am here." While slowly and deliberately drawing in your breath, repeat the phrase, "Jesus, I am here." Then, as you let your breath out, say, "I am ready to listen." While slowly and deliberately exhaling, repeat the phrase, "I am ready to listen." This is a simple way of centering yourself in the present moment. The challenge will be to stick with it. But the more you practice this discipline, the more aware you will be of the widening space within you. And into that widening interior space, you'll discover things that Jesus is telling you.

The first-century directive of Jesus' mother echoing forward through the centuries into our twenty-first-century experience begins with silence so we have space to listen. In the stunned silence that followed Travis' diagnosis of testicular cancer, how could we have possibly known that our own response to such centuries-old advice would find its way into an email?

11

Gratitude

"Living lives that are continually steeped in intentional gratitude allows us to see everything from a different perspective—from the perspective of Jesus, who brings something out of nothing, fullness out of emptiness."

—Paul Gauche

During the first few weeks after the cancer diagnosis, Nancy Lee sent an email to both Travis and Sarah to let them know we were committed to walking the difficult road with them. She told them we were committed to loving, supporting, and encouraging them in the journey ahead. But Nancy Lee also wanted to ask Travis what we might specifically do for him, and how we might specifically pray for him.

It was something in Travis's email back to Nancy Lee that became the focus for us during the approaching season of Thanksgiving in the weeks ahead. Here is Travis's response:

Hey, Nancy Lee, thank you so much for checking in and for the encouraging email. We certainly are being challenged in this time, but we are determined not to despair. It is not at all difficult to see the many silver linings in our situation, the constant receiving of the good

with the bad, and to thank God for those things. In fact,
practicing thankfulness has been very helpful to me in
cultivating a positive attitude.

What is most remarkable to me about Travis's email—even
to this day—is the focus on being thankful in the midst of all
circumstances. As a result, the ancient words from the biblical
writer Paul to the original readers of 1 Thessalonians 5:18 came
to life like never before: "Be cheerful no matter what; pray all
the time; thank God no matter what happens. This is the way
God wants you who belong to Christ Jesus to live" (MSG).

What strikes me most about giving thanks in the midst of
life-threatening realities is that it's not only counterintuitive but
also goes contrary to human nature. Intentionally cultivating
a spirit of gratitude is difficult enough—but being thankful in
the face of the threat of a life-threatening disease, being "determined not to despair," looking for "silver linings," and "taking
the good with the bad," can be a rather tall order. But it was
the last line in Travis's email that really impacted me: "In fact,
practicing thankfulness has been very helpful in cultivating a
positive attitude."

The details of the wedding day in Cana are sparse, at best,
and the ancient writer likes it that way. The way John tells his
story (and, again, he is the only one of the four Gospel writers
to tell it) gives the reader the sense that the harder it appears for
Jesus to repair whatever is broken, the better. It seems that for
John, the more challenging the obstacle, the better the story.
The darker the night, the brighter the day. But the important
point here is that this wasn't about repairing anything—it was
about revealing something.

The story John told wasn't merely about changing water
into wine. It was about Jesus revealing himself as the one who

creates transformation. It was about the one who brings some-thing from nothing, who brings fullness out of emptiness. But the timing for all that wasn't quite right—or so we are led to believe. Jesus' seemingly curt response to his mother— "My hour has not yet come"—gives the reader the sense that the crisis in Cana was just going to have to wait. But then, almost as if Jesus began to revel in the challenge as well as the hope set before him, he signaled that his time had, indeed, come, and he walked deeply into the center of this crisis. Nothing was the same after that.

We can only imagine what took place next as Jesus' mother told the catering crew to "do whatever he tells you." The steward of the feast in Cana knew this was a serious situation and that time was of the essence. Once again, John gives us just a few details: we know "there were six stone water jars available for the Jewish rites of purification, each holding twenty or thirty gallons" (John 2:6), a grand total of about 180 gallons of water.

Keep in mind that having enough water at such an event was nearly as important as not running out of wine. Hav-ing enough water and enough wine was an important part of showing hospitality—a central theme in the message of Jesus. We know that Jesus then told the servants to fill the jars with water. But why would he have given that direction? Weren't they already filled, as John writes, for the rites of purification? If they were filled, what had happened to all the precious water? Were the jars empty? If they were, how would the guests have washed their feet, their hands, and their heads as they gathered for the celebration?

We simply don't know. What we do know is what John tells us as the story continues: "Jesus said to them, 'Fill the jars with water.' And they filled them up to the brim" (John 2:7). This is, in the context of growing marriages, a good reminder that sometimes there needs to be an emptying before the filling begins. Maybe it's necessary to remove something that's in the way and taking up room to create new space and new room for something yet to come.

The servants did just as Jesus directed them in the same way they had done what Jesus' mother had told them to do. In the midst of crisis, they were all too happy to take direction from others who knew what they were doing. At this point, the chief steward, aware that the responsibility of fixing this mess was no longer resting entirely on his shoulders, summoned the bridegroom. With a hint of chastisement mixed with disbelief, he suggested the bridegroom should have had at least one other thing on his mind besides his sweet bride—holding back the "good wine" until the guests had become, shall we say, a little fuzzy around the edges.

A rough translation, a really rough paraphrase, might go something like this: "Usually at a big party like this, you go through the really good stuff first—right off the top when everyone is sharp as a tack and on their best game. And then, only then, when the guests are half-in-the-bag, you bring out the Five-Buck Chuck, because at that point hardly anyone can really tell and no one cares." At which point the chief steward cut right to the point, looked the groom right in the eyes, and said, almost incredulously, "You've kept the good wine until now! You've saved the best for last."

It's easy to get lost in all the details, especially when we're left only to speculate. What remains at the end of the story is that Mary tells the kitchen crew to do whatever Jesus tells them to do. And they do it. It's in doing "whatever he tells you to do" that faith is stirred. And where there is faith, of course, there is hope. And when hope takes root, gratitude emerges. And it's through gratitude that we discover a way from the end of ourselves all the way through to the beginning of the miracle.

But how can we learn to be intentional about living out of a spirit of gratitude? Living lives that are continually steeped in intentional gratitude allows us to see everything from a different perspective—from the perspective of Jesus, who brings something out of nothing, fullness out of emptiness. To give thanks in all circumstances—not just when things are going well, as the apostle Paul says—is actually God's will for our lives.

But developing the discipline of gratitude is harder than it seems. As long as life is going well and we're "healthy, wealthy, and wise," being grateful is easy. But how about when life gets tough and every day presents another challenge? The apostle Paul urged Christ followers to "rejoice always" and to "give thanks in all circumstances." But how?

This Love of Ours . . .

Consider the ancient practice of "counting your blessings." This discipline has made a resurgence in recent years by making use of a "blessing bowl" in your home that contains a collection of written reminders of what God is up to in your life, your relationships, and your marriage. On these small scroll-like slips of paper are written accounts of God's presence in your life during difficult times, answers to prayer, and notes of gratitude for God's provision.

During the last few years of Nancy Lee's mom's life, we noticed she was increasingly worried about many things and becoming quite negative. She began to lose sight of the many remarkable things going on in her life and was overwhelmed by her glass-half-empty perspective. So Nancy Lee encouraged her mother to use the blessing bowl as a way of focusing on specific ways that God's faithfulness had sustained her each day.

We got Nancy Lee's mom a special bowl and a bag of rolled-up scrolls of paper, each one tied with a little ribbon. Nancy

Lee encouraged her mom to take a few minutes at the end of each day to just focus on a couple of good things that had taken place and write them down. Pretty soon, Nancy Lee's mom had a bowl full of blessings to which we could not only add but also take a scroll, read it, and be reminded again and again of God's care. Practicing gratitude in this way gave Nancy Lee's mom more contentment, more satisfaction, and more meaning in the last years of her life.

A similar discipline I've encouraged couples to practice involves using a Gratitude App on a smartphone. This can be any number of apps available that provide a way of journaling or simply taking notes. I have an app on my phone called "Day One," which gives me a daily reminder to simply record something in my life for which I am grateful. Every day at about 3:00, I get an alert that reminds me it's time to make note of my gratitude. So I pause and do what's called "priming." I prime the gratitude pump by thinking back over the day and landing on the one thing for which I'm most grateful. I type "gratitude" in my app, and then in a sentence or two, I describe the things for which I am grateful. This can be something as general as, "I'm grateful for my marriage today," or something as specific as, "I'm grateful for the time that Nancy Lee and I spent together this afternoon talking about our family."

This doesn't have to be a monumental journal entry, nor is anything too small or seemingly insignificant to include. Having this kind of running list with me at all times reminds me that God has been faithful in so many ways, and it provides an opportunity for me to express gratitude. Couples who do this report they experience growing in faith; a stronger sense of believing in something bigger than the two of them. They also experience increased hope and the confidence that no matter how difficult things may be at the present moment, things will change and get better. There's an increase in love as they express gratitude for each other, their friends, and their family—their supportive, loving community. And they also experience the power of gratitude—being thankful for the things they have instead of growing resentful over the things they don't have.

The apostle Paul encouraged his readers to "give thanks in all circumstances; for this is the will of God in Christ Jesus for you" (1 Thessalonians 5:18). It is the will of God for us that we learn to give thanks in any and every situation because being grateful, no matter what, drives us back to the one who made us, who knows us, who loves us, who treasures us, and who promises to never let us go, no matter what. In our relationships, when we're driven back into the heart of God—when we're able to see ourselves there, being held in God's amazing, loving grip—it changes everything. By God's grace, we're invited into a more content, deeply satisfying, and meaningful way of living.

As is normal and even expected in life, every couple experiences some kind of challenge that brings them the to the end of themselves. Charlie and Anna had come to the end of themselves before. Much to their deep dismay, they would find their way back again. They, along with countless couples since the beginning of time, had run out of everything. They, like the rest of us, had come to the end of themselves and wondered how they would fix this, take care of that, manage those things, and get through these days.

Coming to the end of ourselves is difficult for each of us because it usually requires we ask for help, admit our weakness, face our fears, and show some vulnerability. It's at that very moment that the mother of Jesus spoke wise words that have echoed throughout history: "Do whatever he tells you."

Sometimes that changes everything.

12

Hope

"There is no remedy to love but to love more."

—Henry David Thoreau, *Journal*

"Are you sitting down?" Stephanie asked. "Because if you aren't, you probably should."

I've been taking phone calls long enough to know that when someone begins a conversation with that question, you should probably just sit down. But I didn't. I like to think I'm ready for anything when people send a warning signal like that.

I should have thought twice.

The writer of the book of Hebrews in the Christian Scriptures reminds us that "faith is the assurance of things hoped for, the conviction of things not seen" (Hebrews 11:1). Well, I have to say that while I generally err on the side of hopefulness, I never really saw this one coming. Neither the first time nor the second.

I had known Alex and his wife, Heidi, for several years. Their two kids were part of a vibrant youth group in our faith community. Heidi had been involved in everything from Bible studies to chaperoning youth trips. She was a strong, insightful, articulate, and compassionate woman. Alex, a quiet, thoughtful, caring man, was respected as an effective leader. He had served on the church board for several years before becoming the chairperson of the board of directors. I enjoyed working with both of them and being part of their circle of friends during the years I served the congregation.

From every indication, Alex and Heidi had it all together. So I was completely taken off-guard to learn their marriage was disintegrating. Several months after I left that congregation, Heidi called to tell me the marriage was "blowing up." Alex had moved out, and they were in crisis mode. All they had experienced together—all they had built over two decades—was coming apart at the seams.

The months that followed were terrible. There were many sleepless nights, and the long days and weeks that followed were marked by a painful unraveling. The months-long process of the tearing apart of the fabric of their marriage—a tapestry of two peoples' lives that had taken twenty-two years to weave together—came to a conclusion. It was an illusion to assume their two kids, Conner and Stephanie, both now in college and living away from home, would be beyond the effects of watching their parent's marriage disintegrate. This was a nightmare, and everyone would pay a price. It was utterly heartbreaking. The two felt hopeless, and with their relationship in shreds, they divorced. Their marriage died. They buried it. It was done.

Three years later, in September, I received the phone call from Stephanie.

"Are you sitting down?" she asked. "Because if you aren't, you probably should."

There was a hint of anticipation in her voice as she told me she had some "really great news" to share with me. Alex, her dad, was getting remarried. I thought I might have to sit down to let the words sink in.

Stephanie must have realized how this news would hit me, because she paused for a moment before she continued. She went on to say that her dad, after all he had been through in those terrible years, had fallen in love again. He had somehow come through the devastation of a disintegrated marriage and allowed himself not only to hope but also to love and be loved again.

"Stephanie, that's just extraordinary news," I said. And it was. But my comments were tempered; they were half-hearted. I still felt grief and loss, because I had more memories of Alex and Heidi together than I did of them apart. It had been difficult for me to grasp they were really ending their marriage. It was beyond what I could process emotionally to suddenly make the emotional shift and rejoice with Stephanie that her dad was getting remarried. But I figured if Alex was happy and Stephanie was happy, there was some hope.

Just as I was catching my breath, so to speak, Stephanie continued, "Well, that's not all. I've got some more news for you. Are you ready?" She began to explain how her mother had also found someone and had fallen in love. Curiously, Stephanie asked again, I suppose just to give me one more chance, "Are you sitting down for this one?"

I just chuckled, at which point she told me her mother was getting remarried as well. That's when I finally sat down.

For the next few minutes, Stephanie and I talked about how happy she had been watching her dad fall in love. It was the hopeful "next step" that she had prayed her dad would be able to take. She also talked about the joy she experienced watching her mother "fall in love all over again."

Then, in that instant, something happened. I think it was when Stephanie said her mom had fallen in love "all over again" that something clicked for me. I don't know if it was the way she said it or the twinkle in her eye that became strangely apparent over the phone. But I realized there was still a missing puzzle piece. Stephanie was still leaving something out—and almost begging me to ask about it.

So I did.

"Stephanie," I said, "is your dad getting remarried . . . to your mom? And is your mom getting remarried to your dad?"

There was pause, and then Stephanie said, "Yes!"

Two months later, I recalled this phone conversation on a Friday evening drive to Stillwater, Minnesota, in the middle of October. I parked my car in front of an old Victorian Bed and Breakfast and went inside to reunite two people who had rediscovered something they were rejoicing in together: the power of hope.

I'll never forget the image of Heidi taking Alex's hands and speaking her promises to him—once again. As she looked deeply into the eyes of the man to whom she had been married for more than two decades, she said softly, "I always knew—I never stopped believing—that you were the man I was going to share the rest of my life with."

As the tears rolled, their life began again.

I will be the first to admit this story is far from common. It is a unique story of real life and beginnings, celebration and crucible, disintegration and brokenness, death and counsel, and healing and hope, which leads back to love. I'll also be the first to admit there are some relationships that should not continue and some marriages that should never have started in the first place. But this story reminds us that hope can be a powerful force in marriage. Relationships take an enormous amount of work. And right along with love, grace, joy, mercy, peace, vulnerability, patience, honesty, kindness, integrity, goodness, faithfulness, gentleness, forgiveness, and self-control—right along with all of that—hope plays a vital role.

But there are times when we feel as if we need a miracle to get through the next week. There are days when we're convinced it's going to take an act of God to get through the next hour. There are moments when we desperately need to be reminded of the hope of the Third Day.

John Ortberg is an author, teacher, and a pastor who writes powerfully about the significance of Scripture's love affair with the Third Day. The use of this phrase, "the third day," is like a golden thread of hope running from one end of the Bible to the other. The Third Day seems to point to a time-in-between-time; a time of waiting for things to change. In story after story in the Bible, people are waiting for help to arrive. They are aching for some escape, renewal, restoration, and reconciliation to set in. People are hoping a rescue is coming.

For instance, Joseph, locked behind bars in an ancient prison, learned in a dream that in three days Pharaoh would release the chief cupbearer and restore him to his job (see Genesis 40:20–22). Joshua, on the shores of the Jordan River, reminded the Israelites that in three days they would cross into the Promised Land (see Joshua 1:11). Esther, the "accidental queen," called the Jewish people to fast with her for three days before going to the king to ask for their freedom (see Esther 4:16). And it's not just another fish story when we read of a reluctant prophet by the name of Jonah who pondered the meaning of life in the "tomb-like" belly of the whale for three days before finally being "delivered" onto the beach. After being thrown up, spewed out, and regurgitated on the sandy beach, he discovered his life was saved, his dreams had been renewed, and his hopes had been restored—and was reminded that sometimes life is very messy (see Jonah 2:10).

The phrase "the third day" is used dozens of times throughout the Jewish and Christian Scriptures. It may be that it's nothing more than an innocent expression meaning a short time to wait for rescue, or for help to arrive, or for deliverance from some challenge. Nevertheless, it is on the third day that God shows up and shows off. Each of these references ultimately point to a way forward—to a way beyond whatever is happening in the here-and-now in our lives, relationships, and marriages. They point to another context, another reality, another moment in time, another day—specifically, "the Day" the apostle Paul writes about in the Scriptures:

> The first thing I did was place before you what was placed so emphatically before me: that the Messiah died for our sins, exactly as Scripture tells it; that he was buried; that he was raised from death on the third day, again exactly as Scripture says; that he presented himself alive to Peter, then to his closest followers, and later to more than five hundred of his followers all at the same time, most of them still around (although a few have since died); that he then spent time with James and the rest of those he commissioned to represent him; and that he finally presented himself alive to me. (1 Corinthians 15:3–8 MSG)

So it shouldn't come as any surprise to us that when we arrive at the wedding in Cana, we learn the celebration took place on "the third day" (John 2:1). By stating this, John sets the wedding in the context of some other event—though we don't know what that event might have been. In one sense, we might be left asking, "The third day from *when*?" However, the apostle Paul has already set the context in relation to the resurrection. From that perspective, every third day is related to the resurrection.

As Christ-followers, the Third Day is central and significant to what we do, who we are, and whose we are. The Third

Day becomes our identity—we have become "Third Day people." God has made us Third Day people because "the Third Day is when prisoners regain their freedom, the hills and mountains shift and move, pathways emerge through rivers, seemingly powerless women stare down mighty kings, and rebellious and even long-forgotten prophets find themselves tossed onto beaches by enormous fish. And it is on the Third Day that stones are rolled away from tombs. It's on the Third Day that a carpenter comes back to life and changes everything.[3]

This Love of Ours . . .

People experience the hope of the Third Day all the time. If you were to ask Alex or Heidi to pinpoint their Third Day, they would probably tell you about that evening in the living room of that old Victorian Bed and Breakfast. They would tell you about that day they experienced the extraordinary reality of hope emerging from hopelessness and the possibility of something they thought was completely impossible.

A Third Day necessarily presumes a first day and, of course, hints at a "day two." But when you're in those long days (and seemingly longer nights) of wondering what the setting sun will bring, or if the sun will even rise on your relationship the next morning, it's difficult to hold on to the hope that rescue is coming. It's difficult to believe that what you're enduring won't last forever, that your prison door will open, that your mountain will shake, that your river will part, or that the stone will roll away from your tomb. When have you experienced these kinds of days? In your relationship, in your marriage, how does the power of the Third Day show up for you? When things seem impossible, what gives you hope? When things seem broken beyond repair, what keeps you going?

Reflect on your own Third Day journey in your marriage and the hope that has emerged from seemingly hopeless moments. Talk about what it is like not to know what lies ahead. Talk about the challenges that have threatened to undermine your marriage and the joys that have overwhelmed you. Recall the tears that have toughened you and the laughter that has loosened you. Consider the headaches that have pounded away on your life together and the ways the heartbreaks have galvanized you as you've pressed on together. How has knowing that you've had each other and that God has had you been just enough to give you the hope to press on together?

The phone call from Stephanie on that September afternoon long ago was just another profound reminder that on the Third Day, God shows up for people who are struggling, waiting, and wondering. On the Third Day, God shows up for people who are hurting, crying, and searching. On the Third Day, God shows up for people who are dreaming, daring, and expecting. On the Third Day, God shows up for Third Day people who are hoping, anticipating, and praying for him to step up, step in, and step forward. On the Third Day, God shows up for Third Day people who are aching for renovation, redemption, renewal, revival, and restoration. On the Third Day, God shows up to fill up all that has run out.

The young couple in Cana—staring at the chief steward, trying to absorb the news that the wine had run out, and wondering how on earth the moment could be restored—held on to a hope that the God of the Third Day was at work among them. Centuries later, the God of the Third Day is still at work. Charlie and Anna knew this as they stood together at the altar on their wedding day, surrounded by family and friends who were also deeply aware this was a couple who had already lived a lifetime of Third Day events.

Section Five

Miracle

Now standing there were six stone water jars . . .

John 2:6

13

Love

"With my last breath, I'll exhale my love for you. I hope it's a cold day, so you can see what you meant to me."

—Jarod Kintz

"Turn left on Morgan Avenue and drive 500 feet. The destination is on your left." It was 9:54 on a Wednesday morning, and Siri had managed to get me this far. The anticipation of what was to come was palpable as I scanned the houses for an address. Suddenly, my memory retreated to an earlier morning.

The eastern sky began to lighten on the morning of July 18 as Charlie and Anna sat together on the steps outside the chapel. A remarkable celebration awaited them in the day ahead. Anna rested her head on Charlie's shoulder, and after a few quiet moments, some whispered conversation, a prayer, and a kiss, they made their way back to the car. It wouldn't be long before they would return with their families and friends.

At 10:00 AM, Charlie quickly glanced at his watch as he loaded a suitcase, a garment bag, a cooler of ice, and bottled water into his car. He laughed to himself at how quickly he had deviated from the carefully crafted agenda for the morning. Within a half hour, Charlie and his best man arrived at the church and parked the car, just as Anna and her maid of honor arrived. Laughter spilled out of both cars as the four emerged with dresses on hangers, a suitcase with changes of clothing, a duffle bag containing makeup, a box of corsages, boutonnieres, and ribbons for the decorations.

Charlie walked from the car to the front door of the chapel with a spring in his step that matched that of any other young groom anywhere. He paused there to wait for his bride. Anna walked with grace and great expectation for the day ahead. There was more than enough thrill to go around on this mid-morning in July, and it could have easily been said that spring was bursting out all over. Most of it was in Anna's youthful step.

But the spring in Anna's step betrayed her age. The same was true for Charlie. On this bright, summer morning, Anna was all of seventy years of age and then some. But no one would have known it as she looked into the beaming face of her handsome groom, Charlie, now just beyond his eightieth year.

Charlie opened the door to the chapel and reached out to take Anna's hand. In this one moment, they realized that what seemed, at one point in their lives, completely impossible was now a reality. They were sure of things once hoped for and convinced of things previously unseen. And in this moment that seemed more poetic than words could convey, Charlie took Anna's hand as she stepped close to meet his kiss. Together, they took their first precious steps into the chapel on their wedding day, engaged in a marriage that had already begun.

Anna was born ten years before Charlie, which means that together they had more than 150 years of life experience together. Combining the years of their previous marriages, they had just over 110 years of married life between them. The ages of their children and grandchildren spanned four decades. Charlie and Anna were not only blending families but also blending stories of growing up on both coasts, attending schools in the Midwest and the Southeast, and falling in and out of love half a dozen times before finding the loves of their lives—for the first time.

Together, yet separately, Charlie and Anna learned from missteps, mistakes, hardships, and heartaches. Each one knew the heartbreak of enduring the death of a spouse and also the joy of finding happiness and contentment in the midst of life. They had both celebrated births, baptisms, confirmations, and graduations. They had planned weddings for their friends, their children, and their grandchildren. And now, finally together, they had planned their own wedding, the second for each. This, indeed, was the day that God had made for them to rejoice and be glad in.

It was now just a few minutes before noon, and the last of the guests to arrive were being seated. Charlie and Anna sat together in a room adjacent to the chapel as the musician played and the candles were lit.

"Just a couple more minutes to go," I said. "Are you both ready?"

Charlie flashed a big smile. "As ready as we'll ever be!" he said.

"Perfect!" I said. "Then let the celebration begin!"

I turned and moved toward the door, thinking again about what I had just said. Turning back toward Charlie and Anna, I corrected myself: "Perfect! Then let the celebration *continue!*"

The wedding ceremony progressed just as we had planned and anticipated. Charlie and Anna's hopes and dreams for this moment, first jotted down on a napkin in a coffee shop, were now playing out before us. But there was one moment that couldn't have been anticipated, planned, or even scripted any better than how it actually played out.

During the message, I drew on the ancient wisdom from the story of the wedding in Cana and talked about the importance of Charlie and Anna not only inviting Christ to their wedding but also to their marriage. I talked about the wisdom of doing whatever Christ tells them to do in the midst of the crises that would certainly come. And I talked about expecting the miracle of water turning to wine in their life and marriage. But to push the image a bit further, I asked Charlie and Anna if they would be willing to help me illustrate this.

Behind me on the small altar were two beautiful, fluted, crystal wine glasses. The first glass was filled with water, the other with wine. I invited Charlie and Anna to drink from the first fluted glass and describe the taste to me. They took turns tasting and passing the glass of water back and forth between them.

"So, Anna," I said, "what does this first one taste like—the glass of water? How would you describe the flavor?"

Anna took another taste and thoughtfully replied, "Plain. . . . It tastes plain to me."

I handed the water glass to Charlie and asked him to taste it and provide a word to describe its flavor.

"It's ordinary," he said, taking another swallow. "It's flat, sort of 'blah.' It's just ordinary."

"So," I continued, "let me make sure we've got this right. The water has a plain, rather common and ordinary taste to it, right?" They both agreed. Perfect.

I took the second glass (the glass of wine), handed it to Anna, and asked her to describe the taste. She used words like "robust," "fruity," "uncommon," and "extraordinary."

Charlie then took the glass, put it to his lips, and tasted it. His face brightened.

"Well, Charlie," I said, "what do you think? How would you describe what's in that glass?"

The room grew quiet with anticipation as we waited for Charlie's response. Charlie looked at me, then looked at his sweet bride, and then looked back at me. He took another deep swallow of the wine, at which point the room erupted into laughter.

"Okay, Charlie," I said, "before it's all gone—before we run out of wine right here and now—how would you describe the taste?"

Charlie paused once more, looked at Anna, and then looked back at me. The room was completely still again, waiting for his response. Charlie took one more sip and announced for all to hear: "Zippy! It's kind of zippy!" The room once more filled with laughter.

Perfect! I thought. *That's just perfect!*

It *was* such a perfect moment. From the youngest to the oldest, we were all awash in the hilarity of this moment filled with laughter—good, healing, deep, honest laughter. Just as Charlie and Anna were surrounded by the laughter in the room, they were also embraced by the deeper wisdom in the ancient story from John. By inviting Jesus to their marriage—by doing whatever he told them to do in the midst of crisis—they could, indeed, experience the robust, uncommon, and even extraordinary miracle of a "zippy" marriage.

This Love of Ours . . .

For the past dozen years, Nancy Lee and I have adopted an annual practice that has truly added a zippy layer to our marriage. Drawing on the resources from Les and Leslie Parrott's *The Love List*, we set aside time each year—usually during a weekend getaway between Thanksgiving and Christmas—to do two things that I recommend to you.

First, we review the past year and each make a list of our "Top Ten Highlights" from the previous twelve months. We review our journals, look back through our calendars, collect photographs, and recall the events that have breathed new life into each of us and brought us closer. It's been great fun to consider both big events, like a cruise to Alaska or a week-long visit to our granddaughters, as well as the seemingly small but nevertheless significant experiences, like our frequent walks with the dog, which has allowed us some great conversations.

After we've talked through our highlights, we turn our sights to the year ahead and chart our course together. This is where we, as the Parrots say, "turn up the volume on our marriage" and get super intentional about creating future highlights. We talk through our dreams and goals and make a list of our "Top Ten Big Dreams." The list we make together includes everything from landscaping and remodeling projects to books and movies we want to read and see together, to more time spent with our family, to growing spiritually together. It all goes on the list of future highlights we want to create together. Then, as we move through the year, Nancy Lee and I return to the list, usually during our weekly Friday morning breakfast together. We discover this adds so much joy to our otherwise zippy marriage.

In the simple act of reviewing your past and looking intentionally toward your future, you can experience the hidden becoming revealed, the mystery becoming known, and the plain becoming exceptional. You can witness Jesus continuing to turn your nothing into something, your common into the uncommon, your routine into the remarkable, and your ordinary into the extraordinary. As I stood at the altar with Charlie and Anna, I realized the miracle had happened yet again. Christ had turned water to wine, the hidden had become revealed, the plain had become exceptional, and the sign had become evident. Jesus had turned nothing into something, the common into the uncommon, the routine into the remarkable, and the ordinary into the extraordinary. Now, even the extraordinary had become, well . . . "zippy!"

14

Reception

"Who, being loved, is poor?"

—Oscar Wilde, *A Woman of No Importance*

"The destination is on your left . . ."

I was suddenly jolted into the present moment. I turned off the street and into the sloping driveway as Siri intoned once more: "You have arrived at your destination." Playfully, I replied, "Thanks again, Siri. I'll take it from here."

I glanced at the address on the house to make sure it matched the address I had written on a piece of paper. In recent weeks, Anna and I had spoken a few times on the phone, but this was the first time I had seen her since her wedding day in mid-summer nearly ten years before.

I walked up the steps to the front door of their 1950 post-war-era home, shifted the backpack on my shoulder, rang the doorbell, and waited. A moment later, the inside door opened. I looked through the glass of the storm door into the face of the beautiful bride who, when we last stood facing each other at the altar in the chapel at Prince of Peace, was standing next to Charlie—the man whom she would call her husband for only seven years.

"Good morning, Anna," I said as she opened the door. "It's so great to see you!"

"Good morning to you too, Paul!" she said. "Please, come in!"

Anna was, on this morning, just as I remembered her on that bright morning nearly a decade ago: delightful, kind, gracious, and welcoming. But she was alone, and had been for some time. Two and a half years earlier, Charlie had lost his battle with Alzheimer's disease. With Anna by his side, he slipped away from her with the same degree of dignity with which he had come into her life.

Memories of their wedding day stirred in my mind as we sat down at the dining room table. The coffee pot gurgled, signaling the last few moments of the brewing cycle. Anna retrieved two cups, some cream, and a plate of banana bread, and then we settled in for a long-overdue conversation. I could feel the warmth of the morning sun as it poured through the window behind me, brightening the face of this lovely woman with such a remarkable story.

Anna had been born in Plainview, Minnesota, sixteen days before Christmas on December 9, 1929, barely two months after the Great Stock Market Crash. On that same day, Charlie was 134 miles away in Frederic, Wisconsin, celebrating his tenth birthday. Neither of them, of course, could have possibly imagined the birthday gift they would become to one another more than seventy years later. But along the way, both Charlie and Anna would come to know the joys and sorrows of life and the chills and challenges of raising a family. Each of them would come to know the remarkable thrill of finding love as well as the devastating heartbreak of loss.

The first of many poignant moments in our conversation took place when Anna reflected on her marriage to her first husband, Steven. This was, without a doubt, the most difficult issue with which she wrestled during our conversation.

"Anna," I said, "can we talk again about how your first husband died?"

During the weeks of marriage preparation leading up to the wedding, I had talked with Charlie and Anna at length about the joys and happiness of their early lives, the steep challenges, and the redemption—the "revaluing"—of their grief and pain. This had provided a helpful, if not healthy, way of framing the new love and excitement that Charlie and Anna were experiencing together. But the grief and pain of a time much earlier in Anna's life seemed to rise back to the top in that one moment.

Anna was focused and looked right at me as the question began to roll out. She knew we would, at some point, talk this through, but even with that expectation, that anticipation, the question seemed to catch her off guard. I knew this would be a painful remembrance and studied her face to look for ways to press in, however gently.

Anna paused and hesitated slightly as my question registered in her mind. Then, in the next moment, even as the words hung in the air, her focus on me seemed to diminish. She was now looking right through me to some other set of images in her mind. The door to a hidden vault of memories had been flung wide open, and she was suddenly far away in some utterly lamentable place. The impact of the images before her seemed to leave her numb.

A moment later, her countenance shifted once again. She looked down at her folded hands on her lap and, for a few quiet moments, pondered her response. Then she slowly lifted her head once again and looked back at me, regaining her focus. For several moments she had been absent, but now she was back. Then she told me, "He took his own life. Steven took his own life."

Anna fell in love the first time with Steven. On September 16, 1950, they celebrated a wedding at Trinity Evangelical Lutheran Church in Elgin, Missouri, and began a marriage that would last more than three decades. In that span of time, they welcomed three children and, along with them, a houseful of activity. But heartache, pain, and devastation also arrived and set a tone for their future together as a family. Anna and Steven welcomed a son, and then two daughters. But at the age of sixteen, their son was severely injured in a car accident. The injury proved too challenging, too heavy, and too difficult for Steven to bear.

"He just never seemed to get over it." Anna told me.

So, after thirty-two years of marriage, Steven "took his own life." Adding pain to heartache, one of two daughters was diagnosed with schizophrenia, a condition that surfaced only after Steven's death. Then, adding devastation to the pain and heartache, Anna's other daughter was diagnosed with breast cancer—and ultimately lost her battle with it.

"It was a hard time in my life," Anna said.

"I can't imagine, Anna." I replied. The two of us sat together in the profound quiet of that moment.

Anna knew she had to be intentional about these dramatic changes in her life. She would root her decision to manage the transition from those deeply difficult days to a life beyond them in her strong faith and trust in a God who had always remained faithful to her. She was also determined to redefine her life on her own terms, rather than being defined by those moments. In order to go forward in a healthy way, she immersed herself in a career.

"Anna," I said at length, "tell me again how you and Charlie met."

Anna discovered all kinds of healthy and courageous ways to move on in her life. And move on she did. She was introduced to Charlie at a health care conference at the Minnesota State Capital in the spring of 2003. There wasn't anything especially memorable about that introduction for either of them, but those simple beginnings provided just enough for both of them to tuck away until the next time they ran into each other.

That "next time" occurred several months later at a volunteer appreciation dinner that Anna attended in the basement of Bethlehem Lutheran Church in Minneapolis. Anna entered the ballroom and looked for a table with an available chair. It was just a few moments later when Anna looked across the room and recognized Charlie. He was already seated, but there was an empty chair beside him. Charlie saw Anna, smiled, and invited her to join him.

Anna would later reveal to her family and close friends that while she talked with a lot of volunteers, she felt particularly comfortable with Charlie. There was something about him that she trusted, something in his gentle manner to which she was drawn.

Charlie had known his own version of joy and sorrow. He had been married to his first wife, Rachel, for forty-five years. They, too, knew the happiness of raising a family and welcomed two children. But grief would overwhelm Charlie, as Rachel suffered a heart attack and died.

Charlie and Anna engaged in spirited conversation at the dinner. They exchanged stories and discovered, of course, that they had both been married, had both raised children, had both worked to support their families, and had both appreciated traveling. But, most intriguingly, they discovered they shared the same birthday. They had been born on the same day, but ten years apart.

A fire had been lit.

After the banquet, on the way out of the church, Charlie told Anna that he had tickets for an upcoming travelogue that was taking place at a local high school auditorium. He asked if she had any interest in going with him to learn about the Baja Peninsula. Anna said "yes," she would love to do that.

Even now, Anna told the story of their date with an easy laughter and a twinkle in her eyes. "We were living in two different cities," she said. "I was living in Burnsville, and Charlie was living in Brooklyn Center. That's a distance of about twenty-five miles. Sometime during the next couple of days, Charlie sent me a note about the travelogue at the high school and some details about our 'first date.' I had told him that I'd drive part way and meet him someplace, and then we would go together. But Charlie insisted on driving down to Burnsville and picking me up at my home. So that's what he did. He drove from Brooklyn Center to Burnsville to pick me up. We then drove all the way back up to Brooklyn Center, to the high school for the presentation on the Baja Peninsula. After that, we drove all the way back down to Burnsville, to bring me home, and then Charlie drove all the way back up to Brooklyn Center. That was our first date. He drove more than a hundred miles! That's quite a commitment!"

This was the first of several dates that would necessitate long-distance driving for Charlie—a task of which he never seemed to tire. Anna recalled that Charlie asked her out to dinner on their first Valentine's Day together. However, he gave no thought about reservations, so when they arrived at the restaurant, they discovered they would have to wait about an hour for a table. "That didn't bother us at all," Anna said. "It was actually a good thing. We just sat together, talked, and got acquainted."

Anna shared that she and Charlie often laughed when they thought about the amount of money he must have spent on gas during those early stages of their relationship. But, she added, "Charlie never said one word about it."

Anna went to retrieve the pot of coffee, returned to the table, and refilled our cups. Then, together, we reminisced about their wedding day.

It had been more than three years since Charlie's first wife, Rachel, had died of a heart attack. It had been more than nine years since Anna's first husband, Steven, had died at his own hands. With more than a decade of re-singleness between them—navigating the sorrows and joys of life without their spouses, at eighty-three and seventy-three years of age, respectively—Charlie and Anna ultimately arrived at a remarkably redemptive day and spoke profound words of commitment and promise to each other in the presence of family and friends.

On that particular day at that particular time in that particular place, Charlie and Anna were as happy and as much in love as any couple I'd married who were a fraction of their ages. They sealed their commitment with a kiss, received the blessing of family and friends, and—with rousing applause—stepped back over and beyond the threshold of that chapel into the journey ahead, knowing that wherever the road led, they would travel it together.

And travel it they did. Their trip to Mackinac Island for their honeymoon was just a warm-up for the journeys they would take together. Just a year into their marriage, and perhaps inspired by the travelogue about the Baja Peninsula they had seen on their first date, Charlie and Anna packed for a ten-day trip to Italy and Switzerland. In the spring of 2006, when Charlie was eighty-six and Anna was seventy-six, they made a

5,000-mile road trip from Minnesota to California and back to visit friends and relatives.

Anna went on to explain, "We split the driving, but for most of the way Charlie was the driver and I was the navigator. It just worked out better that way. It was a really terrific trip together. We saw four national parks and climbed the one hundred steps that overlook Lake Huron."

"Oh, to be young and in love," I said. Anna simply smiled.

But none of those travels would compare with the journey of love that lay before them in the few years that followed.

This Love of Ours . . .

There is something powerful about the memories we make and the history we write as a couple that galvanizes our relationship. Often, when we reflect on our past, the good prevails and the happy memories rise to the top. We don't much like to bring up the challenges and tend not to ponder the hard times, but it's no secret that it's the hard times that galvanize our relationship. Like solder that binds two pieces of metal together, like a weld that fastens iron together, it's the heat and the pressure that teach us the deepest life lessons.

Take some moments together and recall some of the challenges you faced over the past several months. What did they have to teach? What were the life lessons you learned? How did those difficult challenges tear you down? How did they build you up? When you look back over the time you've been together, how have the difficulties added richness to your history together? If you could, what would you wish away? What can you give thanks for, even now?

15

Blessing

"Grow old along with me; the best is yet to be."

—Robert Browning, *Dramatis Personae*

Marriages have framework and movement. Charlie and Anna's life together had its own framework; their beginnings had created a path into the deep joy of celebration. Together, they had embraced the crucible of marriage and had reached out for counsel along the way. Together, they had come to know the miracle of life together.

Through that framework, Charlie and Anna had also experienced movement together. The movement from their first introductions led them into deeper trust, and then on into commitment. They moved from engagement into deeper invitation, and from their ceremony they moved into marriage. Equipped with their promises, they moved through crisis, sought counsel, and heeded advice, which brought them gratitude and gave them hope. The love they experienced in their life together taught them to dance from one anniversary to the next and into the extraordinary experience of life together.

But I wanted to further explore the framework and movement of their life together—to draw out the lessons that Anna was treasuring from her life with Charlie. Certainly, any couple married half as long or who had spent twice the number of years they had together could benefit from it.

"Anna," I said, "I'm wondering if you can share with me the best reason for joy in your marriage to Charlie. What brought you the most happiness with him?"

Anna was thoughtful for a moment and then said, "It was, without a doubt, Charlie's strength of character and his honesty."

"Can you tell me more about that?" I asked.

"When it came to blending our two lives into one," Anna replied, "it was never a challenge. Bringing together 'yours, mine, and ours' was never a challenge for us. As far as finances went, we would just 'settle up once a month.' He was truthful to the core . . ." She stopped and gave an easy laugh. "He was always a reliable partner."

I reminded Anna that on the day she and Charlie were married, her granddaughter Katie read the Scripture passage from John 2. Anna smiled as she recalled the moment. "Christ was certainly present in the joy and celebration of your wedding," I said. "But tell me, how did you and Charlie continue to invite Jesus to your marriage? How did you continue to do whatever Jesus told you to do?"

"Service and devotions," Anna replied. She went on to describe the commitment she and Charlie had made to growing in faith together. One of the ways they accomplished this was by sharing daily devotional readings. She expressed how important it was in their marriage to be frequently connected to the stories of Scripture and talking together about how those stories spoke to their life together. They were not content to let this remain merely a theoretical exercise but were intentional about making their marriage an expression of what they were learning. This took them a step further as they offered themselves in service to others.

I knew we'd be turning a corner in our conversation about Charlie. So I paused a moment and let the silence create some space for what was coming next.

"Anna," I said, "I know this is difficult for you, even now. But can you tell me what the heartache was like in your marriage? What were the crises? Where did you really need Jesus to turn the water into wine in your life with Charlie?"

"Dementia," she replied. "Sundowner's Syndrome."

We both stopped to let it all sink in. Then she continued, "It was the Sundowner's Syndrome. The dementia was the hardest for me, for him, for both of us. All together, it was about four years. It was a very difficult time, even at first, and it just got harder as the time went on. It's almost unbelievable now when I think about it. I wondered how long I could last. As we got closer to the end, I couldn't leave him alone. Charlie was on oxygen, and he had the idea the tank would blow up. I had to hide the tool for adjusting it. I had to monitor and chart all his medicines and prescriptions. Charlie would even put chairs in front of the doors, thinking people were going to break into the house."

When a couple stands together on their wedding day and makes their promises to each other in the company of their community, they can only imagine how the words will fill up with their own life experience and find specific meaning in their life together. "For richer, for poorer . . ." brings its own set of cares and concerns, especially at first. When the marriage is new and a couple is "living on nothing more than butter and love," there is often a sense that together they can handle anything.

"In sickness and in health . . ." seems to go a step further, if not deeper. Couples discover a certain pride in being able to enter into even the most unpleasant of circumstances, caring for each other whenever the flu season rolls around, for instance.

But it's the next step— "until death parts us . . ."—that really creates an awareness of how deeply rooted the commitment is between people.

No couples like to think of death on their wedding day, nor do I suppose they should. But somewhere in the deep recesses of the bride and groom's mind is that profoundly sobering thought, *One of us will stand at the deathbed of the other; one of us will care for the other right into death when it comes.*" For some, perhaps many, this is too weighty a thought. The love and tenderness in an early-stage marriage can't conceive of such a thing.

But Anna knew she would walk into even more difficult times with Charlie. Yet she knew she wasn't walking alone. She knew the one who had blessed them to be a blessing to each other in life would be faithful to both of them in death. She had known this poignant truth one other time in her life. The second time was coming.

Charlie had been moved to a nursing home not far from where they were living. Anna was with him early on the morning of the day he died. It was sometime around 4:00 AM when she, sleeping in a chair adjacent to Charlie's bed, woke up and looked over at the man she loved so much. She didn't know what it was, really, that caused her to get out of the chair and walk over to where Charlie lay sleeping. But she did. And after a brief moment standing there, she quietly, gently, crawled onto Charlie's bed and tucked herself in right next to him. She lay there for quite some time, dozing, dreaming, yet aware this was *kairos* time without seconds or minutes.

At some point, one of the nursing staff came into the room to take Charlie's blood pressure. When she finished, she looked at Anna, still lying next to Charlie, and said, "His blood pressure has gone down. He's resting well. He's very much at peace." Hours later, sometime around noon, Charlie's pastor came to see him. He read some of the Scripture passages that were marked in Charlie's Bible as Anna listened quietly. Anna recalls that being a comforting time, especially after hearing the verses Charlie had marked in his Bible—verses and passages that he and Anna had read together over the previous few years.

Sometime around 2:30 in the afternoon on Wednesday, September 8, 2010, at a nursing home in Brooklyn Park, Minnesota, Charlie took the last of a lifetime of breath. In a quiet moment, just as the afternoon was beginning to lengthen, Charlie slipped away, letting go the treasure of life that God had given him and taking hold of the promise that was always his.

As I sat there at the dining room table, the quiet of Anna's home seemed to embrace us. It was several moments before either of us said anything. The solitude was profound and peaceful as the two of us sat together, surprisingly comfortable with the enormous silence of that moment. Finally, I reached across the table and took hold of Anna's hand. "Thank you," I said. "Thank you for telling me this story."

After several more quiet moments, Anna looked back at me in a way that seemed to deliver a kind of surprise at the strength and confidence she had gained through telling the story. Choosing her words carefully, and speaking them deliberately, she said, "You're welcome. You are very welcome."

Water had been turned to wine yet again. The common had become uncommonly grace filled. The ordinary had become extraordinary. The tasteless had become zippy.

Anna sat back in her chair. "You know," she continued, "the miracle we experienced together has come into sharper focus since Charlie has been gone. If there was a silver lining at all, it was that Charlie's dementia, mercifully, only lasted six weeks. But as I look back on our seven years together, I thank God for so many great gifts—companionship, the loyal friendship, the committed marriage. That was Charlie. If he made a commitment, he kept it. I do miss him; I miss him a lot. I think most of all, I miss the companionship around the house. But I'm so thankful for our wedding; that we had a marriage and a life, and love together. That was the greatest gift of all. That's the greatest gift of all."

I packed up my notes and put them into my backpack. Anna walked me to the door and thanked me for coming. I stepped into the bright morning and made my way down the steps toward my car. It was then I heard her say, as she stood in the doorway, "I can't wait to read your book!"

I paused, looked back, and said, "I can't wait to tell your story!"

Section Six

Benediction

Jesus did this, the first of his signs, in Cana of Galilee, and revealed his glory; and his disciples believed in him.

John 2:11

16

Anniversary

This love of ours, you of my heart, is no light thing;
For I have seen it in the east and in the west,
And I have found it in the cloud and in the clear.

— e e cummings, "Reverie"

It's the last day of September, and I am near the middle of the
second week of a new workout series at the gym. The workouts
are part of a daily commitment I've made to not only get in
great shape but also stay in great shape. I like to think that for
every day I commit to nurturing my physical health and being
intentional about my spiritual and emotional health, there will
be an increased number of days I will have with the woman I
met on the top step of Stub Hall so long ago. It is a day worth
marking. It is a day filled with love, laughter, and joy. But most
of all, it is a day filled with gratitude for the more than three
decades of life we've shared together.

On this day, just like every other September 30 for the past
thirty-four years, I'll make a phone call to my good friend Bill
who, on that bright, new, crisp, colorful Wednesday morning in
the Fall of 1981, said that he had someone he'd like me to meet.
At some point during the phone call, after we've caught up on
other details of life and family and work and play, I'll remind

Bill that I'm really just calling to say thank you. I'm calling to thank him for introducing me to Nancy Lee Johnson. And I'll thank him for being the witness at a wedding for a marriage that has ebbed and flowed and moved from what I've come to know as the movements: introduction to trust, trust to commitment, commitment to engagement, engagement to invitation, invitation to ceremony, ceremony to marriage, marriage to promises, promises to crisis, crisis to advice, advice to gratitude, gratitude to hope, hope to celebration, and celebration to the extraordinary experience of love into life together.

Anniversaries are important moments for you and your spouse to once again ground yourselves in the joy that first brought you together. Whether you've been together three weeks and four days or thirty-four years, it's essential for people in relationships, in marriages, to set aside moments to consider the importance of time together. And really, while time may be fleeting, being together is what makes all the difference. It's in the beauty of being together that you ultimately catch a faint glimpse of what e e cummings must have meant when he wrote, "This love of ours, you of my heart, is no light thing."

"Thanks, Bill," I said.

"You're welcome!" he said. "Hmmm, thirty-four years of marriage, that's amazing! So is the fact that we've been having this little conversation, what, now thirty-four years in a row? That's the kind of stuff you read about in books on marriages." As if teasing—because he knows me well—he added, "Can you recommend a book on relationships?"

After we hung up, I sat for a moment reveling in the deep joy of my relationship with Nancy Lee, our marriage now into its fourth decade. Nancy Lee walked by.

"How's Bill?" she asked.

"He's just great," I replied. "He's just great," I replied. "He sends his love, and he asked how we're doing after all these years!"

"What did you tell him?"

"Well, I told him we're still dancing."

This Love of Ours . . .

Anniversaries are significant moments on the timeline of a relationship. Anniversaries provide opportunities not only for marking the passage of time, but also—and perhaps more importantly—for understanding the meaning of the time together. One of the most rewarding tasks of writing a story, a blog, a book, or even a song is settling on a title. People who pay attention to the "how" of creating titles suggest all kinds of strategies for coming up with catchy ones. These include using numbers, interesting trigger words, robust adjectives, and making promises. Think of your marriage as a beautiful story, a book, a poem, or even a song. What title would you give it? What words would you use to describe the passage and meaning of time you're marking?

17

Dance

*"We knew we had each other, we knew God had us, and
we knew that was enough."*

—Paul Gauche

Her cheek was warm and soft on mine. My eyes were closed,
and I didn't want to move.

But we were dancing, so I was more or less obligated. People
would have talked if we'd just stood there still as fence posts,
awkward as junior high students in the middle of the dance
floor, mesmerized by Bryan Adams belting out his epically popular (if not timeless) ballad, "Heaven." But I didn't much care
at that point. It was heaven—or at least "heavenly"—at that
moment, and I didn't want it to stop.

A few summers ago, Nancy Lee and I had the opportunity
to co-officiate the wedding of the daughter of some dear friends
of ours. The ceremony was a rich mixture of ancient traditions
and contemporary practices. The gathering of friends and family experienced both laughter and tears and created a wonderful
experience of blessing for this young couple.

Their lovely wedding celebration happened to be within
days of our own thirtieth wedding anniversary, which height-
ened our sense of wonder of our own marriage journey. It was

later, during the reception, that a profound sense of wonder and deep gratitude rolled over me. The band, having played several up-tempo rock-and-roll tunes, changed the pace and slowed things down—way down. Nancy Lee and I, already warm from the cardio workout of the previous song set, recognized the melody of the slow tune and decided to continue dancing. I stood in the middle of the dance floor, took Nancy Lee's hands in mine, looked into her sweet face, and asked, rather playfully (if not a little suggestively), "Hey you, wanna dance?"

With a coy smile and a subtle bit of flirtation that has come to define how we've often interacted together—even in public—she replied teasingly, "We already are." I really didn't need to ask, and she certainly didn't need to answer. As she said, we were already dancing, and had been for nearly thirty years—almost to the day.

I held her close, closed my eyes, and felt her warm cheek on mine. As I did, I was flooded with gratitude for the music between us that had kept us dancing together all those years. We had danced to music that played when we had no idea what lay ahead, when we didn't know what joys would overwhelm us, when we didn't know what challenges would undermine us, and when we didn't know what laughter would loosen us or tears would toughen us. We had danced to music that played even as headaches pounded away on us, heartbreaks galvanized us, blessings were multiplied, and sadness was divided.

We had danced to music that, as it played—especially then—always reminded us that even in the face of all we did not know, three things remained: we knew that we had each other, we knew that God has us, and we knew that was enough.

Afterword

Years ago when I began working with couples preparing for marriage, someone said to me, "You should keep track of all the weddings you do in your ministry. Someday you'll be glad you did." At that time I had no idea why I'd be glad, but I did keep track. I am glad I did. And now I know why I did.

Today, I'm still connected to and invested in many of those couples. I'm helping them dance the dance of marriage and strengthen their relationships. I'm equipping them to work through challenges. I'm helping them mark poignant milestones in their lives: births, baptisms, blessings, graduations, weddings, anniversaries, retirements, all manner of changes and transitions, even deaths.

The first wedding at which I officiated took place on an impossibly hot and stifling Saturday afternoon in September 1984. Family and friends gathered together in the stuffy 112-year-old sanctuary of a classic Midwestern Lutheran church without air conditioning. The only saving grace was the collection of electric fans that were strategically placed to accomplish a couple of things: keep the bride cool, and keep the groomsmen from passing out.

Fifty percent isn't bad. The father of the groom made an epic leap from the front pew to catch the seventeen-year-old groomsman just after his eyes rolled back and just before he hit the floor. In the end, the fans worked but did little to prevent some of the guests from gently encouraging me to preach a short wedding message. I reminded them this was my first wedding, and because of that I had no real benchmark for time. After all was said and done, in spite of the summer swelter, it was a beautiful wedding (with an important, if not mercifully, brief message) in a beautiful setting on a beautiful day.

That was just over 400 weddings ago. Every wedding since—from that perfectly executed, albeit uptight and by-the-book ceremony, right up to the most recent, relaxed, joy-filled celebration—has been its own unique and remarkable movement: introduction to trust, trust to commitment, commitment to engagement, engagement to invitation, invitation to ceremony, ceremony to marriage, marriage to promises, promises to crisis, crisis to advice, advice to gratitude, gratitude to hope, hope to celebration, and celebration to the extraordinary experience of love into life together.

If I've learned anything about dancing with Nancy Lee, it's that the faster I dance, the more likely I am to step on her toes. So I've had to learn to slow down—*way* down—and think in terms of two. Because of that, we've learned to dance in time with each other as one.

As you read these pages that have come and gone, I hope you've considered the movement from where you've been to where you're going in your marriage. You've met a few couples along the way who have moved fast, others who have moved slowly, many who have stepped on toes, and some who have stopped moving together . . . altogether. In every case, there's much to learn as you continue to move ahead in the dance.

Paul Gauche
Lervick's Landing, Pelican Lake, 2017

Gratitude

To Nancy Lee, sweet love of my life and partner in the dance for more than thirty-four years: Here's hail to the rest of the journey!

To Sarah and Travis, for being living reminders of what unconditional love, family commitment, and faithfulness to God look like. I love you to the moon and back! Twice.

To Soren Paul, for asking if I knew of any good books on relationships, and for teaching me some of the deepest meanings of fatherhood, friendship, redemption, and renewal. "There's a big world out there—Don't miss it!" I love you, buddy!

To Eugene Peterson, mentor, model, and friend, for sharing several remarkable conversations about pastoring, writing, and tending to the ways that God's Story weaves through our story; and for the book, *The Pastor*, which was the catalyst for this project.

To Bob and Suzanne Lervick and Doug and Grace Schroeder-Scott for extravagant generosity and hospitality which provided remarkable spaces in peaceful places for me to write.

To our parents, Joyce and Gene Gauche and Grace and Duff Johnson, whose marriages provided more than a hundred years of combined modeling for long-lasting, loving marriages.

To my team of readers and editors and all who dutifully waded through early versions of the manuscript, providing feedback, perspective and encouragement that kept pushing the project forward: Scott Albers, Julie Anderson, Beth Beaty, Beth Bouman,

Jen Cockerill, Mark DeVries, Nancy Going, Brian Goke, Craig Hillier, Jason Kramme, Mike Lemmage, Bob McIntyre, Rich and Arlyce Melheim, Jess Olson, Kyle Peterson, Tim Ramey, Terri Sharkey, Nancy Jo Sullivan, Matt and Kathy Valan, and others whom I can no longer recall at this point who gave me just what I needed just when I needed it--you know who you are;

To Cara and Mike Lemmage for committed friendship and honest modeling of what it means to make and keep promises;

To Jen Cockerill, Lisa Gustafson, Wendy Horton, Kyle Peterson for creativity and wild enthusiasm in promoting "The Dance" so that so many can learn to "Keep In Step";

To Jeff Marian, my dear friend and colleague whose passion for Christ, strong leadership in the church, and constant encouragement brings me great joy and challenges me to always be a better version of myself;

To the staff, my friends, and the wider community of faith at Prince of Peace Lutheran Church in Burnsville, Minnesota, for over two decades of amazing, joyful, grace-filled years of love, hoopla, and hilarity in the midst of change and transition;

To my friends at Deep River Books: Bill and Nancie Carmichael for years of friendship and an enthusiastic welcome into the family of published writers; to Andy Carmichael, Tamara Barnet, Crystal Vogt, Alexis Miller, and Mark Weising for their insight, patience, and guidance through the process of turning something pretty good into something really good;

To all the people in this story, both named and unnamed, and especially every one of the over 400 couples I've had the privilege of working with to make good relationships better and great marriages stronger;

Finally, to Orwoll and Gladys Aalgaard Olson for inviting me to their wedding dance and the rest of us into the "Dance" of their remarkable marriage story.

Endnotes

1. A.W. Tozer, *The Pursuit of God: The Human Thirst for the Divine* (Camp Hill, Pa. Christian Publications, Inc., 1982), p. 77.

2. Brian McLaren, *We Make the Road by Walking: A Year-Long Quest for Spiritual Formation, Reorientation, and Activation* (New York: Jericho Books, 2014), p. 172.

3. John Ortberg, Kevin Harney, and Sherry Harney, *Old Testament Challenge, Volume 2: Stepping Out in Faith Teaching Guide* (Grand Rapids, Mich.: Zondervan/Willow Creek Association, 2003), p. 19.

Connect with the author at:

pgauche@popmn.org

www.paulgauche.com